KRIS KRISTOFFERSON

Tempo
A Rowman & Littlefield Music Series on Rock, Pop, and Culture

Series Editor: Scott Calhoun

Tempo: A Rowman & Littlefield Music Series on Rock, Pop, and Culture offers titles that explore rock and popular music through the lens of social and cultural history, revealing the dynamic relationship between musicians, music, and their milieu. Like other major art forms, rock and pop music comment on their cultural, political, and even economic situation, reflecting the technological advances, psychological concerns, religious feelings, and artistic trends of their times. Contributions to the **Tempo** series are the ideal introduction to major pop and rock artists and genres.

Bob Dylan: American Troubadour, by Donald Brown
Bon Jovi: America's Ultimate Band, by Margaret Olson
British Invasion: The Crosscurrents of Musical Influence, by Simon Philo
Bruce Springsteen: American Poet and Prophet, by Donald L. Deardorff II
The Clash: The Only Band That Mattered, by Sean Egan
Kris Kristofferson: Country Highwayman, by Mary G. Hurd
Patti Smith: America's Punk Rock Rhapsodist, by Eric Wendell
Paul Simon: An American Tune, by Cornel Bonca
Ska: The Rhythm of Liberation, by Heather Augustyn

KRIS KRISTOFFERSON

Country Highwayman

Mary G. Hurd

ROWMAN & LITTLEFIELD
Lanham • Boulder • New York • London

Published by Rowman & Littlefield
A wholly owned subsidiary of The Rowman & Littlefield Publishing Group,
Inc.
4501 Forbes Boulevard, Suite 200, Lanham, Maryland 20706
www.rowman.com

Unit A, Whitacre Mews, 26-34 Stannary Street, London SE11 4AB

British Library Cataloguing in Publication Information Available

Library of Congress Cataloging-in-Publication Data

Hurd, Mary G.
  Kris Kristofferson : Country Highwayman / Mary G. Hurd.
  pages cm – (Tempo : a Rowman & Littlefield music series on rock, pop, and culture)
  Includes bibliographical references.
  ISBN 978-0-8108-8820-3 (cloth : alk. paper) – ISBN 978-0-8108-8821-0 (ebook)
  1. Kristofferson, Kris. 2. Composers–United States–Biography. 3. Singers–United
States–Biography. I. Title.
  ML420.K93H87 2015
  782.421642092–dc23 [B]
  2014048511

∞ ™ The paper used in this publication meets the minimum requirements of
American National Standard for Information Sciences Permanence of Paper
for Printed Library Materials, ANSI/NISO Z39.48-1992.

Printed in the United States of America

For my husband Charles;
daughters Ellen, Donna, and Sarah;
son-in-law Cliff;
grandchildren Merritt, Emily, and Forrest;
and Fred, Gracie, and Charlie

CONTENTS

SERIES EDITOR'S FOREWORD

Kris Kristofferson: Country Music's Highwayman

The real facts of many of America's country music singer-songwriters' lives were once their own, and they brought them to Nashville in the 1960s and 1970s to turn them into lyrics, music, and recording and performing careers. Kris Kristofferson is one such example—and an extraordinary one at that—of an artist whose life could easily be told in a country music song full of what are now the genre's own clichés, left by the deep impressions Kristofferson and a small group of artists like him made. Having a hard-living, hard-luck story to overcome, he did so with grit and guts and then wrote about it with the finesse and sensitivity of a Romantic poet, which we might think of as stereotypically ill suited to surviving the world of country music in its early decades. But this is some of the paradox of Kristofferson's career. As an army veteran who had enough military service to speak from experience about the aftermath of military service, as a son rejected by his own family, and as an Oxford-educated balladeer, he brought the wealth of a troubled spirit and gifted mind to a Nashville that took him in but could not remain a home for him.

More of the Kristofferson paradox is that while he became one of country music's greatest songwriters, he struggled to find similar acclaim as a performer of his own songs. Though he had a significant hand in evolving the genre to encompass the introspective, plaintive song style that was short on rhyming and classic hooks, he was outpaced by the changes in the country music scene, as each successive iteration of Nashville artists after Kristofferson drove the genre to merge onto the interstate of American popular music. In studying Kristofferson's twin careers in music and acting, the two roads he has traveled as a kind of Homeric outlaw, we are afforded a view of the changing culture of the country music industry itself. Its stars are asked to burn brighter and brighter and find a way to be a voice of both protest and celebration without sacrificing commercial appeal. It's enough of a balancing act to prompt some artists to look for safety in clichéd phrases and themes of heartbreak, the comforts of friends and family, or of finding the freedom to live on one's own terms and with the gusto of man's best friend. Kristofferson's never been one to play it so safely, though, which is how a troubled spirit travels, and in his case arrives as a musical icon of Americana.

Scott Calhoun

ACKNOWLEDGMENTS

I would like to acknowledge the assistance and advice of Ellen Markland and Stuart Thayer, and thank them for their help.

INTRODUCTION

Not too long ago, I was delighted to see Kris Kristofferson in concert at the Civic Coliseum in Asheville, North Carolina. He was appearing with Merle Haggard, who had top billing, as part of a tour that extended for several months over three continents. Since I was preparing to write this book, the event was fortuitous. When the lights came up and he walked on stage to a warm welcome, I marveled that he appeared much younger than seventy-six; and when I heard the familiar craggy voice, I remembered that nearly five hundred artists have recorded his songs, many of them timeless classics, because of the musical public's disdain for his voice.

He opened with "Shipwrecked in the Eighties," a favorite with veterans that depicts the U.S. government's neglect of the Vietnam veterans following their service to their country, as well as a painfully low ebb in Kristofferson's own life. As he continued through the concert, singing unforgettable songs he had written more than forty years earlier, I found myself lost in contemplating the twists and turns of his songwriting career since he first visited Nashville in 1965. Kristofferson seemed as unsuitable for traditional country music as he may appear to be for a part in this series. As his father was a major general in the U.S. Air Force, he was clearly intended for a life of military service that was put on hold for his Rhodes scholarship studies; and after three tours of duty in the U.S. Army, it was rejected to pursue a career in songwriting. Well educated, worldly and liberal, he felt sympathy for the plain, hardworking people as well as the disadvantaged, and saw the conservative, country music genre as the only place he could express his raw, honest emotions. "There had never been a country songwriter quite like him," says country music historian Bill C. Malone (305).

Brimming with the ideas about communication through emotion from the nineteenth-century English Romantic poets, the directives of William Blake regarding the fulfillment of one's talent, and the lyrics of Hank Williams coursing through his psyche fifteen years after he first heard him, he was desperate to express himself. While on leave from the army, he visited Nashville, and upon returning home, he resigned his commission. A mecca of songwriting, Nashville was the source of the renewal he felt following his brief association with creative songwriters he met there. But furious at his rejection of their values, his parents disowned him, bringing about his enormous alienation from them and the society he lived in. He threw himself into writing about his loneliness and alienation, his own need to express himself merging with the counterculture's need to express itself in the face of authoritarianism. He adopted an almost militant defense of his personal freedom.

This book follows his songs over a period of more than forty-five years, beginning with the first creative burst that took away the collective breath of the musical public with its forthright, intense, lyrical expressions of the most basic human emotions. It ends by marking his singular comeback, at age seventy, and after several years of recording inactivity, with *This Old Road* and two succeeding albums that he says help "make sense" out of the end of his life. But in between the beginning and the near end of his extraordinary songwriting career is the evolving complexity of a unique individual. This book attempts to explain the different facets of Kris Kristofferson—rebellious son of military family, outspoken lyricist of loneliness and alienation, countercultural icon, film actor, sex symbol, and tireless human rights activist—and their interactions with his songs. After the success of his first album, *Kristofferson*, produced by Fred Foster at Monument Records in Nashville, he became known as a country music singer. He began touring, and with his obsession with freedom, it is little wonder that Kristofferson was enchanted with the road. Perhaps while moving around as a military family when he was young he learned to love journeying, or more likely traveling satisfied a need for new experiences. In a bygone era, he might well have been a cowboy, establishing connections with the American landscape with all its vast space, loneliness, mystical beauty, and spirituality. "I love the road," he has said. Willie Nelson, in "On the Road," has extolled the joys of "making music with [his] friends" and imitating a "band of gypsies." Nelson's song suggests a need to escape from the conformity of mainstream existence and welcome the freedom of new experiences, certainly a source of enjoyment for Kristofferson as well, and not only in the physical sense. Some of his earliest influences, the Beat poets, sought inspiration and liberation from conformity in a country whose materialistic and prudish values they could not accept, and wrote some shocking poetry designed to show their liberation from the confines of convention. Jack Kerouac, who defined the Beat generation and wrote *On the Road*, spent most of his life roaming the country—an activity he considered a priority in his life. Kristofferson also found the philosophy of William Blake, his spiritual mentor, invaluable concerning personal freedom from authority.

Likewise rebelling from conformity and authoritarianism in the 1960s were countless young people who "dropped out" of mainstream society and left home to roam across the country; these countercultural persons fled from the hypocrisy viewed in their parent's, that is, the establishment's, behavior to practice the equality and honesty they believed in. Many of these hippies, identified by their long hair and casual attire, admired individuals who broke the rules. And while the hippies had not been welcomed by country music followers at that point, they were becoming familiar with Kristofferson's songs. In their disavowal of mainstream values, they loved his honesty and frank sexual lyrics, and found in him a hero because of his unconventional dress and manner. His rebellious behavior and his defiance of the establishment relating to his struggle for freedom of expression earned him the well-deserved title of countercultural icon.

The road figures prominently in Kristofferson's self-expression, dating from his most widely known song and the one that defines the sixties generation, "Me and Bobby McGee"; the song resonates with his motifs of loneliness and freedom and the unforgettable sentiment: "Freedom's just another word for nothing left to lose." The song of the penniless, rootless lovers, who, during the great social upheaval, hitched rides across the country and became separated, served as the countercultural anthem. His early songs followed paths of intense experience underscoring emotional honesty, sympathy for people on the fringe of society or using their personal freedom to "satisfy a thirst [they] couldn't name," wariness of authority's dishonesty and abuse, and criticism of hypocritical behavior. Individuals are driven by loneliness to desperate attempts at connections with others and face overwhelming loneliness when their relationships end. The singer-songwriter appears as a "walking contradiction," who, battered by experience, failure, and loneliness, discovers that for everything he learns he also learns its opposite, and he takes "every wrong direction on his lonely way back home."

Kristofferson's touring and performing placed him in a changed psychological and emotional state. The songs of raw, direct emotion vanished and in their wake appeared songs of experiences on the road, many of them reflecting his freedom to do as he chose. While critics and reviewers complained of his diminished lyrics, he explained that he was in a different place at that time and would naturally write different songs; he has persisted in writing, touring, and singing—all of which he enjoys. In his most recent album, *Feeling Mortal* (2013), he says, at age seventy-seven, "The highway is where I believe I belong," and looks forward to "losing myself in the soul of the song." Because each song reflects how he felt at the time it was written, all his songs tell the story of him, psychologically and emotionally, and record his changes brought on by experience and the passage of time. He writes of his success and its nightmarish effects upon him and his life (while hinting at the destructive power of self-delusion); he speaks in interviews of his increased drinking on the road to render himself capable of performing before an audience; and he speaks of "breaking every tie" before it binds him.

Kristofferson's journey of self-expression was and still is a spiritual passage. Early in his struggles to become a successful songwriter, as recorded in "To Beat the Devil," he was hungry, cold, and impoverished, and he encountered the devil who tempted him to give up. He resisted, saying he needed to "feed the hunger in [his] soul." Giving up meant denying his talent, and without creativity, the wellspring of his life, he had no reason to go on. From the time he made his fateful decision to pursue songwriting and began his journey in Nashville toward that end, he understood his quest was to discover and define himself. Believing the "devil tempts a hungry man," Kristofferson redoubled his efforts to continue, aware that the devil's function was to prove his mettle. His songs' frequent shadows, usually linked with the devil, convey spiritual seeking, or a sense of trying to find himself by confronting the darkness to take risks or perhaps challenging his own demons along the way. His daredevil drunken helicopter stunts in the army, his larger-than-average number of automobile wrecks, his need to drive himself past the point of exhaustion into a near collapse, and his periodic fits of bleak depression all indicate the existence of a dark side that sought redemption.

As country music singers are perceived as real, as opposed to imposters, largely because of their backgrounds, many have emphasized their bad behavior to lend credibility to their status. Merle Haggard's youthful incarceration certainly seems to authenticate him as someone who has lived the life he sings about. On the other hand, Johnny Cash's phenomenal performances at Folsom and San Quentin Prisons have provided evidence to many who steadfastly believe he was a prisoner despite the fact that his total time in jail amounted to several single nights for minor offenses; in fact, it has been noted that the confusion in some minds adds much to Cash's legendary status. Others, like Dolly Parton, transform their childhood poverty into mythic country music background, and even folk singers generally project poverty and loneliness.

As for Kristofferson, news of his rebelliousness toward authority and the Nashville music establishment provided a genuine aura, as did his drinking and rowdiness. Of those who knew of his level of education and recognized the obvious literary influences in his songwriting, many were astonished by his sophistication. But most captivating is the connection he makes with his audience. His communication of loss, passion, and loneliness resonates with each person, who, in turn, feels the songwriter has lived what he sings and is authentic. And for the true Kristofferson aficionado, his craggy voice belies the slick, easy utterance and lends a ragged expression of true emotion.

Interestingly, one road Kristofferson has traveled throughout his entire career that has become the hallmark of his music is writing songs that reflect what he really believes. In his early songs, his candid songwriting attracted censorship because of the provocative nature of the songs. One particular instance of attempted television censorship was fought off by Johnny Cash, who sang "Sunday Morning Coming Down" on his own program with the original words intact. "When I came here [Nashville], that [telling the truth] is what I came here to do," says

Kristofferson on *Speaking Freely*, a weekly program in Nashville concerning free speech (September 19, 2003). He received an award, the Spirit of Americana Award, sponsored in part by the First Amendment Center. The first recipient of the award was Johnny Cash, partly for his refusal to change Kristofferson's song lyrics.

By the 1980s, Kristofferson's convictions, always mingling with his art, turned toward political issues, specifically the U.S. government's intervention in Central America. Still bristling about the government's dishonesty concerning Vietnam, he believed it was his moral obligation to speak out against the U.S. pretense of removing Communists in Nicaragua as a means to overthrow the country's duly elected government. He wrote two albums of protest, becoming a liberal activist at the same time he was one of the Highwaymen, an extremely popular country music outlaw group. The second album, much grittier and more outspoken than the first, was not marketed by the record company; as a solo recording artist, he was perceived as irrelevant, and his recording career collapsed.

But in 2006, eleven years later and at the age of seventy, Kristofferson made a remarkable comeback. He recorded *This Old Road*, an album fostering a reevaluation of the experiences endured while moving down the road of life and reminding us of the road we are all on. Within the next seven years, he wrote and recorded two more albums in which he faces his mortality. A line on the title track of *Closer to the Bone* says, "Everything is sweeter / closer to the bone"—all very appropriate for someone who has lived, written, and sung songs for a long time. The instrumentation is pared down to the barest of accompaniment—guitar, harmonica, mandolin, and drums—in an intimate setting. In his still craggy and sometimes whispery voice, he speaks of important experiences, life events, and people along the road. In his most recent album, he sings, "I've begun to soon descend like the sun into the sea," but at age seventy-eight, he is still on the road singing and insists he will write songs until "they throw dirt on me."

Kristofferson's long journey of self-expression has also included a career as a film actor that began about the time of his first album in 1970 and, after his appearance in ninety-three films, he is still at work. In fact, there exists an entire generation of people who know him only as an actor. He has worked with an impressive array of directors, including Sam Peckinpah, Martin Scorsese, Paul Mazursky, Alan Rudolph,

Alan J. Pakula, and Michael Ritchie. In 1976, he costarred with Barbra Streisand in the third remake of *A Star Is Born*, which despite its negative reviews by critics, was enormously popular and successful. He played in more starring roles until the ill-fated *Heaven's Gate* (1980, Michael Cimino), whose overruns almost bankrupted United Artists and made pariahs of most of those connected with it. Eventually, Kristofferson was signed for playing a major role in *Amerika*, a paranoid fantasy series premised upon the following idea: what if the United States had been defeated in World War II? Finally, in 1996, he was chosen by indie director John Sayles for the part of a vile, sadistic sheriff in *Lone Star*. While the role was neither glamorous nor lucrative, he was widely applauded for demonstrating a range of character acting no one had anticipated. His role as Abraham Whistler, vampire tracker, in the *Blade* series, originating in Marvel Comics, has a cult following. His most recent film is *Dolphin Tale II*, released in 2014. His songs have been used on countless sound tracks, and for many other films, he has written original music.

I wrote this book out of a long fascination with Kristofferson's songs, and it provided a motive for listening to all of them again. There is no authorized biography as Kristofferson has for some time planned to write his own memoirs or autobiography. There is one unauthorized biography.

This book is intended for anyone interested in Kris Kristofferson and focuses primarily on his songwriting. The reader will find basic biographical information, incidental information about his films, and critical information about his songwriting and his songs. Kristofferson's identification on his passport is "writer," an indication of how he has always seen himself. He says, "None of the other stuff would ever have happened if it wasn't for the songwriting. I've come to appreciate how special a song is compared to other art forms, because you can carry it around in your head and your heart and it remains part of you" (Patterson, 1–2).

I

BEGINNINGS AND INFLUENCES

"So Pick Up That Guitar, Go Break a Heart"

On June 22, 1936, Kristoffer Kristofferson was welcomed into this world in Brownsville, Texas, a town situated across the Rio Grande River from Matamoros, Mexico. At the southernmost tip of Texas, Brownsville serves as a jumping-off point into the world beyond the United States and as a vast port of entry from that world back into the United States. It is a place of boundaries, and its history is marked by disputes, incursions, and battles, having come into existence as a defensive position amidst territorial aggression. Kristofferson enjoyed his early years in Brownsville immersed in Mexican customs and music; raised by a Hispanic nanny and speaking Spanish before English, he only gradually became aware of the anti-Hispanic sentiments in Brownsville. But although he remembers his life there fondly, it is tempting to imagine that through some fantastic feat of cultural osmosis, he may well have absorbed the area's unquiet past inasmuch as a considerable portion of his existence beyond Brownsville has hinged upon his refusal to observe certain boundaries.

It was not that he rejected boundaries arbitrarily; it was perhaps that he understood his own boundaries more clearly. Long before his celebrated phrase in "The Pilgrim" had become known, Kristofferson himself was a "walking contradiction" who did not fit into categories readily, least of all those that had been assigned to him. At his birth, family, tradition, and country formed the bedrock of his existence and established prime boundaries, but the deepest inspirations of his life—the need to create and the desire to help others—breathed in him as a child in Brownsville. "From the time I knew what one was, I wanted to be a creative person," Kristofferson has said (Balchunas, 1). "I Hate Your Ugly Face," an anti-romantic ditty he "made up" (since it was not written down) at the age of eleven in Brownsville, is included in *Closer to the Bone* (2009), an album he recorded sixty-two years later and after more than forty successful years as a singer-songwriter; and his passion for creativity is still undimmed. "South Texas seemed like the Garden of Eden," he says. "I loved the flowers and the orchards and the ruby-red grapefruits." He credits his years in the Rio Grande valley with "teaching him how to see the world" (Pipkin), including his early perception of Anglo prejudice in Brownsville that laid the groundwork for his human rights activism that continued all of his life. He recalls, "I had a definite sense of things when they weren't right. Down in Brownsville, there was a lot of prejudice against the Mexicans at that time. It was an atmosphere that my mother, God bless her, taught me was wrong" (Balchunas, 1). His sensitivity to the American condescension to Hispanics in Brownsville may well be seen as the origin of his songs of protest against the U.S. intervention in Central America in 1986. In fact, from an early age, his sympathies extended toward the downtrodden and the victims of injustice.

Kristofferson's father, Henry, the son of a Swedish immigrant, was a senior pilot with Pan American in 1941. The following year he began active duty in the U.S. Army and was promoted to full colonel two years later. In 1950, Colonel Kristofferson accepted a post with the newly created U.S. Air Force, ultimately attaining the rank of major general. His mother, Mary Ann Ashbrook Kristofferson, also descended from a military family. Her father, a colonel, lost an eye during his service in the Spanish-American War; her grandfather fought in the Civil War, and an ancestor had served in the Revolutionary War. Kristofferson was expected to continue the family's military tradition.

Eventually the family settled in San Mateo, California, a convenient location for the three children to attend school and for the father's new position with the U.S. Air Force. Kristofferson was enrolled in San Mateo High School where his love of football increased, and he won numerous honors in that sport while lettering in athletics. A very popular student, he was voted by his classmates to committees whose authority helped govern the school and was elected to various positions in the student body. His love of literature was worthy of note as was his interest in creative writing and his affinity for the music of Hank Williams, the gifted but troubled country music singer who died of drug-induced heart failure in 1953 at the age of twenty-nine. He first heard Williams on the Grand Ole Opry radio network around the age of thirteen and was stunned by Williams's spectacular cover of "Lovesick Blues," the huge country hit that launched Williams into the country music stratosphere and assured him a spot on the Grand Ole Opry. Williams's inimitable yodeling in the line "Lord, I love to hear her when she calls me sweet da-a-a-dy" wafted across the vast coverage area on Saturday nights. "I bought every 78 he made," Kristofferson remembered in 1999. "He was never played on the radio. He was too strong for the popular salad at the time" (Bowman, 2).

Kristofferson's biographer, Stephen Miller, indicates there was no suggestion that Kristofferson's parents were musically gifted, going on to say that Kristofferson had once said there was no encouragement toward music in the family. He had recalled a time in the fifties, when he was singing with his brother and sister "against their will . . . they'd been told they couldn't sing, and while my sister managed to fake it pretty well, it turned out my brother could carry a tune, so we harmonized on some Everly Brothers things" (22).

Miller also speaks of Kristofferson's own youthful preferences, noting he was a "fan of Buddy Holly and the close backup harmonies on his records, which were provided by a vocal group called the Picks. Nearer to home he drank in the exuberant Tex-Mex music, with its simple melodies and vibrant harmonies, which were part of the local environment" (22). As an army brat, however, Kristofferson was open to a great variety of music and, according to Miller, had not become strongly attracted to any regional style. He says Kristofferson's "preference was invariably for music with the simplicity and lyrical directness of genres such as country and blues" (22).

In 1954, Kristofferson enrolled in his mother's alma mater, Pomona College. A foremost liberal arts college at Claremont, California, Pomona offered him the opportunity to play football and study literature. While his smallish stature and his inability to run fast had prevented him from earning a scholarship from more prominent schools, he excelled in athletic activities at Pomona. He lettered in football, played rugby, and became a Golden Gloves boxer—gaining the respect of his coaches and teammates. "I loved football before I loved music. I could lose myself in it," Kristofferson said. "The closest I've come to knowing myself is in losing myself" (Carrier, 2).

He also expanded his interests and talents, becoming editor of the college yearbook and the college newspaper; he was inducted into the men's honor society as well as Phi Beta Kappa, an academic honor society recognizing excellence in the undergraduate arts and sciences. In addition to these activities and his courses, he found time to write fiction; to an *Atlantic Monthly* collegiate competition, he submitted four short stories, winning first and third place, with two honorable mentions.

But these stories were pieces of a life plan nourished by Kristofferson that ran contrary to the one his parents had devised for him. Following his success with the *Atlantic Monthly*, his professors encouraged him to apply for a Rhodes scholarship. Reluctantly he agreed, but as time approached for the interviews, he balked, and his characteristic shyness and disinclination to speak up resulted in an unsatisfactory first round. He wished to withdraw from consideration, but his philosophy professor, Dr. Frederick Sontag, mentor and friend for fifty years, spent most of the night convincing him not to give up. He was successful in the next round of interviews and was awarded the scholarship (Miller, 31–34).

Straight Arrow (his college nickname) performed very well throughout his college years and participated in Reserve Officers' Training Corp as he prepared for living the distinguished military life his proud parents had planned for him. But he was tantalized by a creative impulse that refused to subside; the more involved he became with literature, especially the English Romantic poets, the more intent he was on living a creative life. The contradictions in his nature, so prominent in his contemplation of the life he wanted, had been present throughout his life in the choices he had made; and, despite his enormous popularity, he had been plagued since childhood with a sense of "separateness" (Burke, "Kristofferson's Talking Blues," 1:25). A classmate at Pomona College comments,

> We always thought he'd do something big; he was president of his freshman class, sophomore class, *every* class, the debating team,

writing club, football team, baseball. . . . Kris was the most respected, best liked guy the school ever had. He could have been president of the country if he'd run but there was always something *else* about him, nice as he was . . . a sadness. In a funny way, I wasn't surprised we didn't hear from him again. (Burke, "Kristofferson's Talking Blues," 1:26)

After earning his BA degree in creative writing from Pomona College, Kristofferson asked for a deferment of his military service and traveled to Oxford University to begin his study of literature. At Oxford's Merton College, he relished the opportunity to spend most of his days in libraries. While he delved into Shakespeare, another English author, William Blake, became an "explosion" in his mind, as some of Blake's expressions from 150 years earlier proved to be the elixir his creative soul had craved. He wrote a novel that was rejected. He met Paul Lincoln, Australian owner of the famous 21's Coffee Bar in Soho, who cosponsored a contest that Kristofferson entered, submitting a demo containing songs he had written and recorded. He recalled, "I found a manager over there. I just answered an ad in the newspaper that said, 'Just dial F-A-M-E'" (Bowman, 1). Lincoln chose Kristofferson as the winner and provided him with producer Tony Hatch and a recording contract with Top Rank Records, headed by British industrialist J. Arthur Rank. He was promoted as Kris Carson, probably with Kit Carson, American frontiersman, in mind. Kristofferson surmised that as a Yank at Oxford, he may have been thought by Lincoln to be "commercially possible" (Bowman, 1). He recorded four folk songs from his original ones similar to songs sung by the Kingston Trio. During that time, interest in the Yank Rhodes scholar singer increased, and an article about him, "The Old Oxonian Blues," appeared in *Time* (April 1959). However, it turned out that Kristofferson had signed a speculative contract earlier with a Los Angeles man, who threatened to sue. Attempts at negotiation were begun, but the individual was adamant; consequently, as Rank wanted no litigation, he never released the recording.

Although Kristofferson was not perceived as the athlete he was at Pomona and was discouraged from trying out for rugby, he achieved excellent grades in philosophy. And despite the rebuffs he endured at Merton College, he enjoyed most of it. In 1995, remembering the freedom he had, he said (as quoted by Miller),

> I was in a wonderful position at the time. I was boxing and playing rugby and seeing places I'd never seen before and reading people I'd never read before. William Blake was an explosion in my mind, and Shakespeare—I fell in love with literature and reading.
>
> American education at this time didn't allow you to specialize enough, especially for someone as lazy as I am, to really do the reading. You had to do the reading. You had to do economics and philosophy and if you did extracurricular activities such as football you didn't have enough time. At Oxford I had to go to two tutorials a week but I didn't have to go to lectures—I could live in libraries. (36)

The fiascoes of his efforts with his novel and album convinced him to back away from his creative ambitions for a while. Midway through his second year at Merton, he returned home; on February 11, 1961, he married Frances Beer, his high school girlfriend and fellow Pomona College graduate, and assuming military life was inevitable, gloomily resumed his commission as second lieutenant in the U.S. Army. But neither Ranger School nor becoming a helicopter pilot (he was a member of the elite Airborne Rangers) could inhibit his dreams of creativity. At this time, his mood was black. He has said that the first day he drove on the military base, "it was like driving into hell" (Burke, "Kristofferson's Talking Blues," 1:24).

He and other musically oriented soldiers formed a band, "The Losers," who played some of Kristofferson's songs in service clubs and bars in Germany. "I was writing the songs since I was a little kid," said Kristofferson, "and I wasn't going to stop just because I wasn't selling them" (Cooper, 1). The band played indecent parodies of popular songs, while Kristofferson turned his songwriting ability toward Hank Williams–style revisions of widely known songs to reflect on his own experience. One of these, "Sky King" (imitative of Jimmy Dean's "Big Bad John"), a satiric look at his flight instructor, who was "about as broad at the shoulders as he was at the hips," consistently shows up in concert performances more than forty years later.

He continued to agonize over his future and his inability to choose the profession he craved. He was miserable, drunk, and unproductive: "I touched bottom," he remembered. "I hadn't written a song in years. When I was smashed it seemed clear I would never write one, nor a novel, nor much of anything, so I drank more. It was very rough, especially on my wife. When you're not doing what you think you should in life, you take it out on your old lady, or whoever" (Burke, "Kristoffer-son's Talking Blues," 1:24). And although he came to understand that the only way he was "going to be able to be a creative person was to be a songwriter" (Cooper, 1), he soon had, in addition to his parents' expec-tations, family obligations to wrestle with, as in early 1962 Fran gave birth to a baby girl, Tracy. He has frequently related his conversation with a general with whom he flew and to whom he revealed his unhap-py situation: "I told him . . . I wanted to be a songwriter. I'm sure it sounded like I'd said I wanted to be Bozo the Clown. But, he looked at me and he said, 'You know, follow your heart.' . . . It was surprising advice to come from a military man. But he knew where my heart was" (Balchunas, 2). At another time, Kristofferson spoke with his platoon commander about his musical ambitions, and his commander suggested he send samples of his songs to his cousin, a songwriter who lived and worked in Nashville. He contacted the woman, who turned out to be Marijohn Wilkin, noted songwriter and music publisher. Wilkin and Kristofferson corresponded, and she encouraged him to stop by and see her if he ever came to Nashville.

In 1965, at the end of his third tour of duty in Germany, Kristoffer-son, having been promoted to captain, was destined for reassignment to teach English literature at West Point and was on track to be promoted to major in less than two years. Once on leave, he said, "I just got crazy. Instead of going to Fran, I got on a plane for Nashville, still in uniform. It was my first time there; everybody called me 'Captain'" (Burke, "Kristofferson's Talking Blues," 1:24). At Buckhorn Music, Wilkin, a producer as well as a songwriter who had cowritten the country music classic "The Long Black Veil" and others, introduced him to Bobby Bare and songwriters Billy Swan and Chris Gantry, who happened to be in her office. Wilkin took Kristofferson to Ryman Auditorium for his first glimpse of his idol, Johnny Cash. Of this life-altering event, Kristof-ferson has said, "He took my breath away. He was the most exciting . . . performer I had ever seen; he was skinny as a snake, wearing all black, and was . . . electrically all wired-up. . . . He was just barely in control, but he was the most driven, gifted, exhilarating and self-destructive artist that I'd seen, and I wanted to be exactly like him" (*Kris Kristoffer-son: His Life and Work*). Wilkin and Kristofferson visited Cowboy Jack Clement, a songwriter and producer renowned for his encouragement of young musicians. Clement, of course, proceeded to present him to every singer in sight, usually "somebody I'd listened to since I was little," said Kristofferson (Streissguth, 15). Later, he took him back to Ryman Auditorium and introduced him to Johnny Cash, who next to Hank Williams was the single most important musical force in Kristofferson's life. Shaking hands with Cash was "like shaking hands with lightning. But he was what I imagined Hank Williams was like," said Kristofferson (Streissguth, 15). Clement introduced Kristofferson to others in the music industry and then took him to the house of Audrey Williams, Hank's widow, where he happened to witness Cajun singer Doug Kershaw, hawking the rights to his hit "Louisiana Man," with Clement declining the offer. Clement then took him "down to the train station because he just loved trains. He'd get on them and ride to New Orleans and back, just to write" (Streissguth, 15). It was a magical day for Kristofferson: "I think," he said, "I probably right then decided I was coming back here. It was so much, that little Professional Club, those two streets, the whole shooting match was right there" (Streissguth, 15).

The exciting first day flowed into two thrilling weeks of little sleep, as new acquaintances filled his ears with music and a great deal of talk about it, while introducing him to all the favorite musical haunts in Nashville. Some of those new folks he met became lifelong friends. He felt like his long-repressed creativity, the primary inspiration of his life, was very near finding an outlet and it lay not at West Point but in Nashville. "In Nashville," he said, "the life had come back into me" (Burke, "Kristofferson's Talking Blues," 1:25).

When he returned home, he resigned his commission. The shock wave that ran through his family rocked his life, investing him with a profound sense of alienation that, along with his already deep-seated feelings of separateness, colored his existence and his music for the greater part of his life. His mother pronounced him a disgrace and demanded he keep away from all family members and friends. He was essentially disowned. Fran, having been accustomed to being treated as an officer's wife, was appalled at living in a $50-a-month cold-water flat with a husband who brought . . . shady people into the house," Kristofferson said. "She didn't want them in the house, let alone have me hanging out with them for three days and nights at a time" (Cooper, 2). Several years later, Marijohn Wilkin recalled, "I felt so sorry for his wife. She came here a Captain's wife and ended up a janitor's wife. The spouses don't understand that we don't have a choice" (Self, 33–34).

Wilkin, who was "teaching school in Tulsa when [she] knew [she] had to write" (Self, 27), continues about Kristofferson,

> The word *desire* is not strong enough. I understand that in people. Kris had to write. He *had* to write. I think his obsession was even worse than mine, because he also needed to be a star. . . . And he wanted to sing worse than anybody I ever heard. . . . He wanted to sing in my vocal group. . . . And he's still singing. The man has to sing. And he had to write. (Self, 33)

Four years and another child later (a son, Kris, born in 1968), the marriage ended. "The music came to be for her kind of a wall between us," he said (Cooper, 2). "You know, it was a time when I just had to be selfish," Kristofferson continued. "Looking back, I was selfish. If I hadn't been, I never would have been able to put up with the hardship I was causing other people. I had a little girl I wasn't seeing much of. And for my wife, it must have been miserable" (Cooper, 3).

His fight for the freedom to follow his own life's work became a life and death struggle to succeed at that life's work. He threw everything he had into meeting, listening, and talking with other songwriters who fed off each other through encouragement and competition. He learned about the recording business, and he worked at menial jobs, including bartender or janitor at Columbia Recording Studio, that kept him in contact with songwriters and recording artists. And primarily, in this best of creative worlds, he applied his own creative powers freely to writing songs, a ritual that, notwithstanding his close association with other songwriters, he always carried out alone.

Kristofferson became a known and sought-after quantity by the musical public when his songs, recorded by other artists, attracted huge numbers of admirers who insisted on having more of them—and when the country music industry acknowledged him, after a five-year struggle, as a major success by awarding him the Country Music Award of 1970 for one of those songs, "Sunday Morning Coming Down," sung by Johnny Cash. That same year he signed a ten-year recording contract with Monument Records that essentially charted the next ten years of his life.

He and his band, the Borderlords, logged an inestimable number of miles crossing and recrossing the United States and the borders into Canada, Europe, Japan, Scandinavia, Australia, and New Zealand. In addition to this, he had become involved in film acting, a move that also exacted considerable chunks of his time, and while it supplemented his income when record sales were lean, it left him short on time for writing new songs to meet his contract provisions. And he sank into the habits of alcohol, drugs, and women that consumed any spare time he might have, adding to his exhaustion and nearly wrecking his life.

By the end of the decade and the end of his contract, he had reached a low period in both personal and professional endeavors. He faced a second divorce and the loss of several of his longtime associates. As the divorce proceedings dragged on, Kristofferson began an NBC television miniseries, *Freedom Road*, starring Mohammed Ali as a former slave and Gideon Jackson, who enters politics to pursue civil rights and, almost unbelievably, becomes a senator. Kristofferson, portraying a poor sharecropper, had benefitted from his years of acting and was moving up to play the starring role in Michael Cimino's *Heaven's Gate* (1980), a film that crashed from excessive expectations, taking Cimino's, Kristofferson's, and several other film careers with it. The 1980s were disastrous for Kristofferson on various fronts, and he began digging slowly out of the ruins. He proceeded to take coparenting responsibilities for his child with Rita Coolidge very seriously, to work on mending relationships with his two children with Fran Beer, and in getting himself sober. After a while he was offered small parts in films, largely made-for-TV films and somewhat controversial films, but, bit by bit, his film roles developed in a widely diverse manner that has supplied him with parts he has enjoyed for an additional thirty-five years.

The end of his contract with Monument coincided with threats of the company's collapse from financial difficulties, and artists connected with it recorded albums to boost its sales. Kristofferson sang on collaborative albums, and Monument issued Kristofferson compilation albums. Other artists sang his songs, doing quite well of course, but his most recent solo albums had not fared very well.

Kristofferson's pairing up with Willie Nelson in *Songwriter*, the film about Nelson's experiences, was very successful, as was Kristofferson and Nelson's union with Waylon Jennings and Johnny Cash, all of them performing as the Highwaymen. This association lasted for a period of ten years, during which time it produced three albums, all warranting extensive touring and rejuvenated the careers of all four musicians. However his political activism, in the form of protest songs, while not damaging the success of the Highwaymen recordings and tours, enraged much of his own conservative fan base. Radio stations refused to play the records, he had no solo recordings for six years, and his musical career appeared to be defunct.

Kristofferson eventually reconnected with Don Was, producer of the final Highwaymen album, who produced some of Kristofferson's more recent songs in a manner that focuses on his most recognizable feature—his voice. In 2006, *This Old Road*, the first of three albums, appeared with stripped-down, minimalist backing that pushes his voice up front and center. The gravel voice, having aged and mellowed, delivers songs about the end of life in an honest, simplistic appraisal of where he has been and where he is going. Sometimes sinking to a whisper, the direct, plaintive voice, in the manner of an ancient troubadour, relates his experiences and ponders his existence much as he had done with a different voice forty years earlier.

The arc of Kristofferson's creative output begins with a spate of intense, contemplative songs of great depth and passion, and moves through a long stretch of songs that generally lack the comforting familiarity of his classics but communicate experiences of life on the road and essentially provide a record of his internal changes. It later makes a left turn into political activism rife with anger and bitterness, but during the first decade of the twenty-first century, the arc of his body of work returns to intense meditations on mortality.

MUSICAL INFLUENCES

The kinship Kristofferson sensed with Hank Williams may well have been his first real identification with any music, considering the disparity between his family's status, with its presumptions and obligations, and his own sensitivities. Not only did he not care for the pop singers his peers idolized, but also he seemed to be strongly attracted to the music of the dispossessed and the anguished. Kristofferson recognized the pain and loneliness in Williams's voice as an expression of the "separateness" that had hounded him since early childhood. Paul Hemphill, Williams's biographer, who was also thirteen when he first heard Williams, thought he sounded like a hurt animal (5). The raw, naked emotion present in Williams's melancholy voice embodied for Kristofferson the long-sought utterances of his own feelings and became his exemplar for expressing his own range of emotions. This plaintive voice, with limited backing associated with Hank Williams and also used so widely and frequently by other singers, has become the earmark of pure country music, famously designated by composer Harlan Howard and others as "three chords and the truth."

The true extent of Williams's influence upon Kristofferson is, of course, incalculable. The sensibility of Williams's desolate "I'm So Lonesome I Could Cry" is woven into "Help Me Make It through the Night," "Sunday Morning Coming Down," and most likely into all other Kristofferson songs expressing loneliness. He was fond of Williams's talking songs, in which his alter ego, Luke the Drifter, sings or recites religious stories about various characters as he wanders from place to place. Williams sings the songs anonymously in order to avoid disturbing the marketability of his more popular songs. Interestingly, Kristofferson's story songs, although not sung anonymously, depict individual characters whose sharply etched lives go tragically awry, or who are victims of inner turmoil or injustice. Kristofferson's receptivity to the emotion in Williams's singing voice stimulates similar feelings in his own songs, creating shadows of sadness and inexpressible longing that resonate throughout.

Although Kristofferson idolized Johnny Cash, he was one of a great many singers who found Bob Dylan a huge inspiration. During Kristofferson's tenure as janitor at the Columbia Recording Studio in Nashville, Dylan was there recording *Blonde on Blonde* (1966). Forbidden to approach Dylan (as was everyone but his staff and musicians), he "saw Dylan sitting out in the middle of the studio at the piano, writing all night long by himself. Dark glasses on. All the musicians played cards or Ping-Pong while he was out there writing" (Bowman, 3). After completion, in the early morning, Dylan summoned the band and recorded the song to perfection. As much as Kristofferson was in awe of the creative process, witnessing it in the hands of a master brought a satisfaction he had only dreamed of. He names Dylan an influence and cites "I'll Be Your Baby Tonight" as a song he had listened to frequently before he wrote "Help Me Make It through the Night." Dylan's most significant benefit to Kristofferson was the fact that despite Dylan's less-than-perfect voice, he sang his own songs and was welcomed by the musical public. Kristofferson reasoned, "Thanks to people like Dylan . . . I could do my own stuff because a voice that doesn't fit into a groove can be accepted doing original material" (Miller, 50).

Kristofferson's fellow musicians in Nashville wielded considerable influence in the creative department. They were all actively engaged in songwriting and would get together regularly and sing what they had most recently written. Mickey Newbury, famous for having written "I Just Dropped In (To See What Condition My Condition Was In)" and "San Francisco's Mable Joy," probably had, says Kristofferson, "more effect on my songwriting than any of my other friends or contemporaries. . . . I was blown away by his songs and his singing . . . [not just] the simplicity of the songs, but [also] how powerful they were. I can see his influence in the songs of mine that were breakthroughs" (Cooper, 7). He and Newbury tossed ideas to one another and listened together to various songwriters' lyrics and techniques for inspiration. Newbury was the first of his fellow musicians to perceive that Kristofferson's real accomplishment in singing lay in his ability to communicate.

The debt of gratitude Kristofferson felt was owed to the songwriters/ singers who were his idols and heroes and to his songwriting companions who struggled alongside him as they all learned together is expressed eloquently. To the songwriters and singers who had flourished before him or during his time, he offered sincere praise and admiration. Once, when watching Willie Nelson on stage, he was so moved by his masterful performance that he wrote "Final Attraction," which merges Nelson with every great musician (Kristofferson included) who has become an artist. Thinking of Hank Williams, and many others whom he names, he offers a tribute to the singer-songwriter artist, who was once "dared into feeling" and is now beloved of his following "for sharing their sorrows; in his finest performances, the artist takes up his guitar and sets out to "go break a heart."

LITERARY INFLUENCES

Kristofferson was enthralled by the nineteenth-century English Romantic poets, becoming first attached to their works while at Pomona and later seeing them as models for his own compositions. He was influenced notably by William Wordsworth's view of poetry as expressed in *Lyrical Ballads* (1800) and illustrated in his poems. Wordsworth's belief

that poetry results from the "spontaneous overflow of powerful feelings" (240) connected with Kristofferson's own intense emotions, ensuring that his songs bear enduring witness to Romanticism. With exceptional artistry, his lyrics plumb the depths of loneliness and alienation and delineate inner turmoil while achieving new levels of expression. "I have always written what I have felt strongly about," says Kristofferson (Leigh, 1), whose earnest assertion may in some way account
for his amazing ability to connect emotionally with large groups of people. Having understood from listening to Hank Williams that songs
could convey yearning in a way unequalled by any other medium, Kristofferson saw the communication and reciprocation of his powerful
feelings as his primary goal. The strength of his convictions seemed to
confirm he had lived his music, and his authentic humanity linked him
with audiences who understood his "passions of the heart" (Wordsworth, 239). He once remarked that "when you're communicating,
when the people out there are feeling the same way you felt when you
wrote the song, that's what makes it meaningful" (Balchunas, 4).

Kristofferson's strongest literary influence had long been William
Blake, nineteenth-century poet, engraver, artist, and visionary, with
whom he had been fascinated at Pomona and whose writings he had
explored at Merton College, Oxford. Kristofferson discovered that
Blake, despite living a seemingly normal life, held quite radical opinions
including advocating freedom from oppressive authority and established religion, and believing that man should look for God not on altars
but within himself. Blake insisted that organized religion suppresses
natural desires and deters earthy pleasure. Although Blake remained,
by all accounts, happily married to one wife, he professed devotion to
the idea of free love, maintaining that marriage vows of chastity were
cruel, sharing the views of others of the "free love" type of thinking that
marriage was only "legalized prostitution." Kristofferson was not the
only person who had studied the writings of Blake and was captivated
by his unfettered reasoning; in fact, Blake's free love stance had been
adopted by numerous counterculture advocates in the 1960s as a linch-
pin in their argument against hypocritical values. Rebellious singer/
songwriter/poet Jim Morrison and the musicians in the Doors took their
band's name from the title of Aldous Huxley's book *The Doors of Perception*, itself a reference to Blake's declaration in *The Marriage of
Heaven and Hell* that "if the doors of perception were cleansed, every-

thing would appear to man as it is, infinite" (154). Within the "Proverbs of Hell," also in *The Marriage of Heaven and Hell* and intended to jolt the reader out of a commonplace idea of good and evil, are epigrams such as "The Road of Excess leads to the Palace of Wisdom" and "If the fool persists in his folly, he will become wise" (150–51)—both of which were cited frequently in Kristofferson's responses to questions concerning his behavior.

But the writings that galvanized Kristofferson are to be found in Blake's 1802 letter to his friend, Thomas Butts, that concerned the artist and his obligation to his art. Firing Kristofferson's consciousness and leaving him a changed person thenceforth were the words he continues to quote into his seventies: "If he who is organized by the divine for spiritual communion, refuse and bury his talent in the earth, even though he should want natural bread, sorrow and desperation will pursue him throughout life, and after death, shame and confusion are faced to eternity" (Blake, 813). Kristofferson took to heart Blake's injunction concerning the moral obligation of the artist to develop his talent.

While from another place and time, the writings of Joseph Campbell, well-known mythologist and author of numerous books on comparative mythology, were influences on Kristofferson and his undecided lifework. Campbell's stories of the commonality of myths and specifically his comments relating to the hero's journey, or the journey we all take through life, emphasize that "each person can have his own depth, experience, and some conviction of being in touch with . . . his own being through consciousness and bliss." Frequently, Campbell questions the good in life if "you've never done the thing you wanted to do in all your life." He explains the phrase "following your bliss," essentially a summation of his philosophy, as follows: "If you follow your bliss, you put yourself on a kind of track that has been there all the while, waiting for you, and the life that you ought to be living is the one that you are living. Wherever you are—if you are following your bliss, you are enjoying that refreshment, that life within you, all the time" (Campbell, 117–20).

In his continuous quest for liberation, both physical and spiritual, Kristofferson found in the Beat poets during the early 1950s inspiration and affirmation of the need to challenge social conformity. The founders, Allen Ginsberg and Jack Kerouac, both at Columbia University in the 1940s, were later connected with Neal Cassady, Lawrence Ferlinghetti, Gary Snyder, and William S. Burroughs, who opposed the post–World War II rampant materialism, consumer culture, and strait-laced priggishness of their parents' generation. They advocated a more expressive existence geared to freer speech and sexuality, use of hallu-cinogenic drugs to elevate consciousness, and the practice of meditation and the study of Eastern religion and Buddhism. Their poetic writing styles defied convention by dispensing with traditional formality in favor of improvisation or jazz techniques, calculated to irk the establishment. Ginsberg's book *Howl* (1956), victorious in its court battle over obscen-ity, implied an unofficial sanction of a freer range of expression without challenge, as did Burroughs's *Naked Lunch* (1960), also the subject of an obscenity battle, and Kerouac's *On the Road* (1963). Like Kristoffer-son, Ginsberg claimed William Blake as a primary influence in his life and work, as he proceeded to exert enormous influence upon rock singers, including the Beatles, who adapted their name from the Beat poets. In their emphasis upon social nonconformity, the Beats also gave impetus to the countercultural movement, although, as a whole, it was less well educated and less sophisticated.

Kristofferson's early songs utilize poetic, elegant phrasing as well as careful attention to syllable and line length and the pattern of accents. As art and culture critic Dave Hickey puts it,

> Kristofferson uses all the skill, knowledge and tricks he learned from studying the great English poets to write those long, perfectly metri-cal, tightly structured quarter-note lines of twelve and sixteen syl-lables, double your standard country line length. They are so tight and clear that it is like having another rhythm instrument in the band. Unlike most country lines, they are trochaic, the accent falling on the first four, or three syllables very heavily. (30)

Besides the long lines, Kristofferson uses distinctive rhyming pat-terns—almost all lines rhyme at the ends, and many feature internal rhyme, where certain words rhyme within the same line. In "Me and Bobby McGee," he rhymes "Busted flat in Baton Rouge"; and "The Pilgrim, Chapter 33," declares, "He's a walking contradiction, partly truth and partly fiction," and contains sixteen syllable lines, numerous internal rhymes, and a considerable use of assonance, or the repetition of similar vowel sounds. The alliteratively hissing line "That silver tongued devil just slipped from the shadows" ("The Silver Tongued

Devil") and "And you still can hear me singin' to the people who don't listen," from "To Beat the Devil," utilize words that nearly rhyme, indicating the wide use of literary devices throughout his songs. Varied literary devices and striking imagery in his peculiar fusion of abstract and concrete imagery, and his desire to effect a realistic change in the ways in which emotions and relationships were viewed and expressed in song, eventually prompted a reconstruction of music in Nashville.

CULTURAL INFLUENCES

The world that Kristofferson felt an urgency to get moving in was not the same world in which his parents grew up, met, fell in love, married, had children, and sought to transmit to those children the same values that had guided them successfully through their lives. Massive changes were already in progress that would leave traditional beliefs forever altered. In 1965, opposition to the Vietnam War was kindling conspicuous protests, mostly among the young, but by 1969 protests against the war shrouded in government deception and demanding increasingly more recruits had divided the country's loyalties and its faith in governmental authority and its foundations. In the previous tumultuous year, the Civil Rights Act prohibiting discrimination in schools, public places, and employment had been passed, and in 1965, the National Voting Rights Act—legislation that followed years of racial segregation and division—became law. The struggle for equality that ultimately included all minority, women's, and gay rights was largely supported by the younger population, who were quite vocal about the entrenched attitudes of their parents' generation as they sought to break free of their roots. Intense concern with social issues influenced countercultural developments that typified ideals running counter to timeworn yet rigidly revered aspects of American culture. Some groups removed themselves to distant communes and lived off the land and according to their own values. Others, voicing their beliefs in change through protest and song, confronted the middle-class bulwarks of authority, morality, and discipline, behind which they saw hypocrisy, inequity, and a denial of personal freedom.

Folk music, the most powerful music of the 1960s, was energized essentially by the Kingston Trio and its 1958 recording of "Tom Dooley," an old North Carolina murder ballad that topped the nation's popular-music hits chart and set in motion the folk music revival. While earlier folk songs from the dark days of the Great Depression had tended to be more radical through their utilization as political weapons, the folk music of the early sixties began with its own radical element in Woody Guthrie, Cisco Houston, and Pete Seeger during World War II. By the late 1940s, folk music inched closer to popular music as the Weavers' "Goodnight Irene" climbed up the popular music chart, and by the sixties, urban folk music attracted a broad spectrum of followers. But the popular spirit of its early performers, such as Burl Ives and Josh White—Kristofferson remembered "having a lot of Josh White albums" (Bowman, 3)—and the host of Kingston Trio imitators had, by the middle of the sixties, been overshadowed by singers at the forefront of the antiwar and civil rights movement (Malone and Neal, 278–79). Prominently numbered as leaders in those protest activities were Pete Seeger, Phil Ochs, Joan Baez, and Bob Dylan, who insists in his autobiography that he was not a protest singer but a "folk musician" (116).

Kristofferson was not part of the antiwar movement—despite having heard some disquieting reports—primarily because he was still close to the army; his brother was a navy fighter pilot in Vietnam, and he had friends in service there. Nor did he actively protest for civil rights. Yet, from his status as disaffected son, evolved a link with things countercultural that proliferated through the intermingling of his own sensibilities and with his experiences in Nashville: his passion for personal freedom erupted from the severe struggle with his family; his pursuit of creative freedom contended with the Music Row establishment's suppression of his outspoken song lyrics; and his distrust of authority was incited by learning of the many police forces harassing hippies, minorities, and the poor, right up to the U.S. government's false statements about its intentions in Vietnam and later on in its aims in Central America as well as its hypocritical stand on the oppressed and the disadvantaged. He insisted on his right to self-destruct through uninhibited indulgence in drugs and sex. Disconnected from his family and under no obligation to continue their values, he grew weary of respect for established institutions, composing antiestablishment songs exposing rampant injustice and hypocrisy. He asserted his freedom, insisting he had "nothing left to lose," meaning that he was autonomous and free to do as he chose. So, with no real misgivings about the past or future, he felt liberated and ready to bring to life and validity the songs that had labored so long to be born.

2

"FREEDOM'S JUST ANOTHER WORD FOR NOTHING LEFT TO LOSE"

1965–1970

Being disowned by his family was certainly a blow, but Kristofferson soon came to appreciate its liberating aspects. While his ageless line about freedom that is the title of this chapter was still some four years in the future, he understood the feeling. No longer needing to please his family or the army, he could now pursue songwriting—the only activity he felt would allow him to express himself. And since he was already twenty-nine years old, the age at which Hank Williams died, he felt it was unquestionably time to become a creative person.

In 1965, Nashville's country music scene was enjoying a resurgence of traditional hard country music, following its previous dalliances with rockabilly, the urban folk movement, and its convergence with country-pop. Singer-songwriters Harlan Howard, Johnny Cash, George Jones, Merle Haggard, and Willie Nelson, who have since become legendary, were turning out songs signaling nostalgic returns to the heartaches of working-class people. And while these gifted musicians were not all staunchly conservative, the majority of the powerful on Music Row, the name given to the two-street business district of the country music industry, was conservative. This tightly knit, controlling enterprise maintained artists whose records sold numbered in the millions, con-veying Nashville country music far beyond America's borders. Into this bustling repository of inexhaustible dreams walked Kris Kristofferson—liberal, worldly, well educated, compassionate, and hungry.

Kristofferson has, on many occasions, reiterated his belief that Nashville was his salvation, in that it represented an opportunity for him to express himself creatively. In the heaven of Nashville, his creative expression burst forth, and he wrote five songs (nothing memorable, by his own account) the first week he was there. "It was incredible," he said. "I'd never seen so many colorful people. It felt so creative to me there. Everybody was creating, writing stuff, every day, and singing it that night at somebody's apartment" (Cooper, 1). Despite the fact that his demo tape consisted of poetry against a background of Hank Williams–type music, Wilkin was the first in Nashville to recognize his potential and signed him to her own fledgling music publishing house, Buckhorn Music, on Music Row. As the recipient of an unpretentious weekly sum that supplemented other money he might earn, he could devote more time toward associating with other struggling songwriters who offered one another support and competition. The first Kristofferson song that Wilkin placed was "Talkin' Vietnam Blues," a right-wing promilitary attack on antiwar demonstrators who had asked him to sign a statement of sympathy for Ho Chi Minh, leader of North Vietnam. Recorded by Dave Dudley, the song was based on an incident in Washington, D.C., and written on Kristofferson's way to Nashville. His view of the Vietnam War would shift 180 degrees before long.

But Kristofferson's prized freedom, born of his own lack of it, stimulated by William Blake's writings, and supported by his own growing sense of the authoritarian failures of the older generation, proved to be a double-edged sword rendering a checkered path. He wrote in 1967, "Lord, help me to shoulder the burden of freedom," referring to his loss of family and quite possibly to other forfeitures yet to be endured for decisions made in his lifelong struggle for personal freedom. In Nashville, the time necessary to compose songs required sizeable intervals away from work, but work was necessary for the support of a wife and child. The ideal jobs for him were those that would require the least of him yet keep him financially afloat. He tried bartending, construction work, and railroad work, and assumed Billy Swan's old job as engineer's assistant at Columbia Recording Studios in Nashville in the middle of Bob Dylan's sessions for *Blonde on Blonde* in 1966. Musician friends encouraged him, with his credentials, to look for a teaching job, perhaps at Vanderbilt University, but he was not inclined. He wanted no employment that would take him away from writing songs or from associating with people whose speech rhythms he wanted to imitate. As Bill Friskics-Warren points out, "Kristofferson had yet to calibrate the blend of highbrow and lowbrow that would become his stock-in-trade. He had some things to learn, or rather unlearn, before country music audiences, singers and the fans would relate to his songs" (5). He was pleased with his job at Columbia as it allowed him to learn about being a songwriter in Nashville, by observing or talking with musicians, or just listening to their conversations. For $55 a week, he ran errands, swept floors, emptied ashtrays, and functioned as a studio setup man. On busy days, he could watch three or four sessions a day. Johnny Cash spoke of Kristofferson mopping "the hallway outside the studio about 20 times and . . . cutting the glass window as I was singing whatever it was that I was singing" (1).

Although success in Kristofferson's chosen endeavor seemed improbably close at hand, the freedom he enjoyed in the quest of songwriting was regenerating. He and his songwriting friends believed they were artists, and the significance of their achievements would eventually be recognized. This time in his life was for him similar to that fabled era of writers in Paris in the twenties, when personal freedom and creativity ruled the day. He has said the best thing about his years in Nashville while trying to establish himself as a songwriter was that "everybody was in love with the creative part . . . and our hearts and souls were totally committed to the songwriting" (Streissguth, 2). They would meet for all-night guitar pulls where each person would sing one or two of his own songs and then pass the guitar to another songwriter who would do the same; this procedure continued around to the last person, whereupon someone would announce a winner. Occurring primarily because of the shortage of performing venues in Nashville, these activities were extremely competitive, and Kristofferson worked diligently to produce the night's best song. He and his friends indulged in marathon sessions of heady creative activity or "roaring," binging "not just on music and smoke and drink, but on inspiration itself" (Friskics-Warren, 7). Occasionally, several days were devoted to a session. Looking back on these memorable times in "The Show Must Go On" (1984), he wrote, "We used to take about a day and a night / to try to sing up all the soul in sight"—with the intensity of these gatherings blocking out everything else. (Fran, pregnant with their second child, along with their daughter Tracy, had already been packed up and taken back to California by Kristofferson's mother.) This group of songwriters, known locally as the Nashville Underground, included Chris Gantry, Kristofferson's friend, who is quoted by Stephen Miller:

> We all hung out together in the streets for a lot of years and saw each other every day. We used to compare our songs and went through the whole camaraderie that exists between songwriters, like a very exclusive sort of lifestyle—it was an apprenticeship, because we were around some very heavy writers and we all influenced each other because we were all different. The Nashville industry didn't go too much for it at first, and it took us a long time to even be accepted to the point where somebody would even consider recording one of our songs. Then when we did start getting some cuts, they jumped on us as being "the new breed" though we'd actually been there for a long time. (58)

Interestingly, fledgling songwriters were inspired by another element, as Kristofferson recounts:

> We got as much encouragement from guys like Harlan Howard, Hank Cochran, and Willie Nelson as we did from our peers. Harlan's probably had a million million-sellers, yet I know there was no better time of year for him than when he'd have a table full of songwriters around him at a place like the Professional Club—where they had a pinball machine, pool table and a jukebox that everybody would get their record on if they had one out—and they'd be bouncing ideas off one another's heads. (Rensin, 28)

Like numerous other songwriters in Nashville, Kristofferson frequented Sue Brewer's house, at her behest, and labored over his songs. "I was just thrilled to be invited in. . . . It was the first thing that had happened for me," he said. Known by musicians as the Boar's Nest and once a favorite place for Waylon Jennings's band, it was a trendy hangout for people "who were hip but who were kind of the underground." Kristofferson declared, "You had to kind of earn your way into it. If you were a heavy songwriter you could get invited in, and you'd sit there on the floor in one of those empty rooms" (Cooper, 6). Widely known by Nashville musicians, the house was immortalized in a song, "On Susan's

Floor," written by Shel Silverstein and Vince Matthews, Kristofferson's friends, and recorded individually by Gordon Lightfoot and Hank Williams Jr.

Kristofferson devoted a great deal of his spare time to reveling in bars with other musicians, in hopes of seeing and talking with more famous singers; any conversation with Webb Pierce, Hank Cochran, or Willie Nelson would have been priceless. He also spent time with musicians in fields other than country music, learning about the music industry and making friends with people involved in various aspects of the business and not just those he worked with closely. He "learned how to pitch songs, and what sort of money he might expect to make" (Miller, 57), having received so little for "Talkin' Vietnam Blues" and being concerned about how long it might be before he could earn a moderately good income.

When his son was born with a defective esophagus and medical bills were mounting, Kristofferson fell back on his helicopter pilot skills and took a lucrative job with Petroleum Helicopters International out of Lafayette, Louisiana, flying equipment and personnel to and from Lafayette and the offshore petroleum facilities in the Gulf of Mexico. He recalled, "I would work a week down here [Louisiana] for PHI, sitting on an oil platform and flying helicopters. Then I'd go back to Nashville at the end of the week and spend a week up there trying to pitch the songs, then come back down and write songs for another week" (Thibodeaux, C2). Long periods of waiting and flying, always in isolation, provided favorable opportunities for composition, some of which produced prolific results. However, on one of his trips to Lafayette, he reached a new low in his circumstances that powerfully influenced his perception that "freedom's just another word for nothing left to lose." He reflects on this point in his life: "I'd lost my family to years of failing as a songwriter. All I had were bills, child support, and grief. And I was about to get fired for not letting 24 hours go between the throttle and the bottle. It looked like I'd trashed my act. But there was something liberating about it. By not having to live up to people's expectations, I was somehow free" (Langer, 1).

Kristofferson left the Evangeline Motel in the swamps outside Lafayette, and thinking, "I'm on the bottom, can't go any lower," drove his car to the airport and left it. Back in Nashville, he soon learned that three of his songs had been cut and were on their way to becoming hits

(Carrier, 2). The first of a multitude of diverse artists who recorded Kristofferson's songs was Roy Drusky and his smooth crooning of "Jody and the Kid." Jerry Lee Lewis, whose exceptional version of "Help Me Make It through the Night" was always one of Kristofferson's favorites, followed, and then came Roger Miller, whose hobo-hippie take on "Me and Bobby McGee" was similar to his own "King of the Road." Mickey Newbury persuaded Kristofferson to pitch songs to Johnny Cash for his new TV Show. *The Johnny Cash Show*, which ran on the ABC network from 1969 to 1971, made inroads into the conservative bent of Music Row, nudging it toward mainstream. Insisting upon originating the show from Ryman Auditorium in Nashville, the true home of country music, Cash proceeded to schedule a great diversity of musicians, including Bob Dylan, Joni Mitchell, Eric Clapton, Neil Young, Louis Armstrong, and Arlo Guthrie, among others. Cash also played and sang gospel music, declared himself a Christian—outraging ABC—and invited Kristofferson on for two performances. He also exhibited many of the stars in the country music firmament at that time: Merle Haggard, Marty Robbins, George Jones, Roy Acuff, Harlan Howard, Roger Miller, and Roy Clark.

Eager to relay some of his songs to Johnny Cash, he had given demos to Cash's wife, June Carter Cash, to pass on to him. Disinterested, Cash tossed them into the lake on his property. Kristofferson, who had taken a weekend job flying a helicopter for the Tennessee National Guard, landed a helicopter in Cash's yard in a notorious stunt to attract Cash's attention. Cash was impressed sufficiently to invite Kristofferson to his home where other up-and-coming singer-songwriters gathered before a huge blazing fire in his living room. The musicians would participate in a guitar pull, each one singing one of his own songs, and on one extraordinary occasion, the musicians reputedly present were Bob Dylan, with "Lay, Lady, Lay"; Joni Mitchell, "Both Sides Now"; Graham Nash, "Marrakesh Express"; and Kristofferson, "Me and Bobby McGee" (Miller, 75). Cash, whom Kristofferson idolized, recognized his talent and invited him to perform with him at the Newport Folk Festival in the summer of 1969. Cash had also performed at Newport in 1964 and had been the first country singer to "forge an alliance with the folk revival" (Malone and Neal, 282), paving the way for other country musicians to appear at the yearly festival. Kristofferson's appearance at the Newport Folk Festival marked the beginning of a performing career of more than forty years. He had hitchhiked to Rhode Island and spent the night in a church, possibly trying to forget his only other performance which consisted of filling in for a friend one night at Nero's Cactus Canyon, back in Nashville, and being fired after about an hour. The next day, when his name was called, he froze; when his name was called again, and Cash pointed out it was time to be going, he still could not move. Fortunately, Johnny Cash's wife, June Carter Cash, rose to the occasion, yelling, "Get out there!" as she kicked him out on the stage. Headlines in the following day's *New York Times* (July 18, 1969) announced, "Kristofferson takes Newport!" His success in Newport brought forth invitations to participate in workshops on the festival site with James Taylor, Joni Mitchell, Ramblin' Jack Elliott, and the Everly Brothers. He was also invited to participate at the Berkeley Folk Festival and other folk festivals.

After several years with Buckhorn Music and no major successes, Kristofferson considered a move to Combine Music. "I couldn't carry him any longer," Marijohn Wilkin explained. "He hadn't had a hit" (Self, 35). Owner Fred Foster had established Monument Recording Studios separately from Combine and had been successful with Roy Orbison and a young Dolly Parton. Monument's affable director, Bob Beckham, invited musicians and songwriters to his office after hours. Kristofferson remembers, "It was Beckham that changed everything. That office would be, at the end of every day, filled up with songwriters. Good ones. Guys that didn't even write for him, like Mickey, and Shel Silverstein. It was a place where everybody would get at the end of the day, sit and pass the guitar around, try and knock each other out" (Streissguth, 55). Kristofferson's interest in signing up as a songwriter with Monument prompted an audition with Foster. Known for shepherding young songwriters, Foster was surprised to see the right sole on Kristofferson's worn boots flapping loose, and he wrapped his foot with a rubber band. Foster observed, "I don't know what a songwriter was supposed to look like, but he didn't look like one to me, at least not one doing very well." Foster continued, "I just put my formula to work: if you came in wanting me to hear your songs, you'd have to sing four. Anyone might luck up and write one. Can't do it four times." Foster then listened to the gravel-voiced singer with even more amazement: after a lackluster rendition of "To Beat the Devil," Foster said, "I thought, 'Well, that's really a great piece of material. . . .' The next song.

I thought, 'Man, I know there's no way this guy can be this good.' Third
song. And I thought, 'I must be hallucinating. . . .' Nobody has ever
come into my office before or since and laid four classic songs on me.
And then he did 'Jody and the Kid.'" Foster has revealed that the other
two songs Kristofferson sang for him were "The Best of All Possible
Worlds" and "Duvalier's Dream," all of which indicated Kristofferson's
inclination toward the lengthy ballad and sounded very little like typical
Nashville music fare. Foster offered Kristofferson two contracts, one
for songwriter and another for artist. Kristofferson said, "What? . . . I
can't sing! I sound like a frog!" Foster responded, "But a frog that can
communicate" (Streissguth, 55–56). Kristofferson signed a ten-year
contract calling for ten solo albums with original material.

Under Foster's care, songwriters enjoyed his noninterference policy.
Foster said, "You've got to let a flower be a flower. You're going to make
a flower bloom differently than it would normally bloom? I don't think
so. Just nourish it, give it enough fertilizer, water and let it bloom. It will
bloom. Business . . . I can't stand it. Business has ruined many a good
man and woman" (Streissguth, 53).

When his first album, *Kristofferson*, was released in June 1970 and
its songs, despite having been previously recorded by other artists, continued to earn acclaim, Kristofferson hurriedly put together a band for
promoting the songs on tour. He gathered three songwriters from Combine to form a band—Donnie Fritts on keyboard, Dennis Linde on
guitar, and Billy Swan on bass—that was serviceable at best; Fritts
admitted later they could play no licks, "only the melody, the chords"
(Streissguth, 88). Kristofferson's first stop was the Troubadour in Los
Angeles, a place especially nurturing to singer-songwriters of the time.
Drifting into the tradition of the medieval troubadour, who sang invent-
ed poems with a lute expressing his own thoughts and feelings, he
performed at its namesake, the fabled club of singer-songwriters who
made history there, frequently performing with only a guitar or piano
and maintaining the emotionally direct and simple delivery of their
feelings. The singer-songwriters who appeared there regularly, namely,
James Taylor, Carole King, Jackson Browne, David Crosby, Joni Mitchell, Bonnie Raitt, and Kristofferson, emphasized feeling, intimacy, and
humanity, all offered as a kind of balm for the extreme turbulence of
the sixties (*Troubadours* [documentary]).

Although Kristofferson was a singer from Nashville, he was considered alternative country, or by some, a maverick. On this, the first of other visits to the Troubadour, he opened for Linda Ronstadt, singing "Help Me Make It through the Night," an event he still insists launched his career. "This was the place to go in L.A. at the time," says Fritts (Streissguth, 87). Kristofferson, who performed with instrumentation, still managed to captivate his audience with his distinctive intensity and authenticity.

The difficulty in finding a musical niche has haunted Kristofferson throughout his career. He insists that he always had a "pretty broad" audience. "My first performances," he said, "weren't in Nashville; they were . . . in Los Angeles and New York. I really wasn't a country performer in the traditional sense, more like Bob Dylan, so I couldn't get any work until I went outside Nashville and found audiences in these hip clubs" (Jordan). Following his show at the Troubadour, Kristofferson went to the Bitter End in Greenwich Village, a place he loved for its intimacy, and was next in the lineup at the infamous Isle of Wight concert in August with six hundred thousand menacing fans in attendance. Fritts speaks of Kristofferson's surprising success that swept him and the band along, all completely unprepared. They did not arrive back in California until October. Of their tour, Fritts says, "No matter how bad the band sounded—and believe me, we weren't that good—it didn't matter because Kris was singing . . . absolutely brilliant songs" (Streissguth, 88). Of this concert, Kristofferson, who performed alongside Joni Mitchell and Leonard Cohen, remarked,

> I didn't think I had great songs at the time, but for some reason I was immediately taken in as a serious songwriter by these guys. . . . Guys like Gordon Lightfoot and Leonard Cohen were already heroes to us. I had a feeling at the time I started performing that Canada was the best audience I had. I think it was probably because of how much I looked up to Gordon and Leonard Cohen. (Schneider, 2)

Later, when he had made his huge impression on Nashville, he was aware of the dichotomy between the two worlds he inhabited; he complained that he spent half his life trying to live down a "red-neck image" in Los Angeles and New York, and the other half "getting killed" for his sophistication when he returned to Nashville and the south (Rensin, 25). All this, of course, intensified his outsider feelings and contributed to his lifelong sense of not being a part of any group or party. Nevertheless, his songs have always seemed universal, a quality that increased their popularity and propelled them beyond country into categories he had probably not envisioned.

Bookings at the Troubadour introduced Kristofferson to an intrigued West Coast audience that found him unique and open to new possibilities. At one of his concerts, he met Dennis Hopper, who persuaded him to participate in his new film, beginning a career in film that supplemented leaner times in his music endeavors and has continued throughout his life. He also met Janis Joplin and engaged in an intense one-month relationship. Hoping to convince her to record one of his songs, he became entangled in days and nights of endless booze, as his plans to leave were continually thwarted by being too wasted to care about leaving. Besides their musical interests, both were Texans from similarly prosperous backgrounds they had forsaken, and they both were beset with alcohol- and drug-consumption issues as well as their own demons. Kristofferson once said of Joplin,

> I lived with her, slept with her, but it wasn't a love affair. . . . I loved her like a friend. She was very soulful, a passionate person but very childlike to me, a little girl in dress-up clothes. She was an unhappy person. Even though she was fun to be around, she felt that the only thing that made her attractive to the world was her art, her talent, her stardom. And she was intelligent enough to know that it was temporary. (Cartwright, 3–4)

Joplin went on, famously, to record "Me and Bobby McGee," which was released shortly after her untimely death in October 1970, becoming the most successful recording of her career. Her death was a jolt to Kristofferson, and upon first hearing her version of the song, he completely broke down. Later, he affirmed, as was his custom regarding any other artists' renditions of his songs, that he liked her interpretation. But he took exception to her rewrite of the line, changing "Bobby clapping hands" to "Bobby holding his hand in mine," as it destroyed his internal rhyme.

As Kristofferson's quest for personal freedom came at great cost, so did his struggle for creative freedom. The force of his need to create freely exerted an intensity and an unusual straightforwardness that seemed to exasperate Music Row sensibilities. Kristofferson's songs favored patterns of meter and length that did not always fit those of traditional country songs, and he delighted in the occasional tart, abrasive song echoing countercultural attitudes toward hypocrisy. Songs speaking of a "warm and tender body," issuing a plea for someone to "help [him] make it through the night," or savagely satirizing middle-class pretense while parodying a well-known Christian hymn were viewed in Nashville as an embarrassing affront to the values depicted in country music. Although proceeding from his own experience, these songs suggested a society where mores were changing—a phenomenon that had not at that time been embraced by the country music empire. Most country music advocates still valued hard work, family love, and respectability, viewing any effort aimed at innovation as an undermining of traditional values, particularly if advanced by someone presumed to be a hippie. Despite the fact that much of the Nashville music scene was scandalized by Kristofferson's early songs, he insisted that country music should present honest depictions of relationships as well as the desperation begot by loneliness. He believed he was following traditional country music wherein songs explore the human heart and record tales of tangled and conflicted emotions. He saw his songs as similar to the plaintive cries of Hank Williams that echoed across the air waves twenty-one years earlier; and he contended, as William Blake had expounded 150 years previously, that an artist had a moral obligation to develop his talent.

Kristofferson's conception of country music allowed no place for the pop-oriented softer sounds that had recently issued from Nashville. The pop inclination, "inherent in country music's development from the very beginning" (Malone and Neal, 254), according to music historians, had flourished in the late fifties in its triumph over rock and roll. Vocalists including Don Gibson, Jim Reeves, Marty Robbins, and Patsy Cline, all diversely talented, were groomed by Chet Atkins, chief of RCA's country division in Nashville, to appeal to musical audiences beyond country and prosper from the extensive commercial exposure. The music of this time period, known as the "Nashville sound," was called originally the "Chet Atkins compromise," Atkins being a nationally known guitarist who pioneered a three-fingered "middle-of-the-road sound" that retained the country feel but found a broader commercial market. The Nashville sound eliminated steel guitars and fiddles, adding instead a succession of smooth violins and a chorus of backup singers, all utilized for crossover into the lucrative area of popular music (Malone and Neal, 256–64). Kristofferson's arrival in Nashville during the Nashville sound, or countrypolitan period, certainly strengthened his endorsement of country music as the "white man's blues" and rekindled his belief in the need for the pure, direct expression of emotion. And despite objections to his lyrics, he and others like him became part of a dynamic new force that would revive the stagnant sixties and, over the next decade, reinvigorate country music.

Malone speaks of the emergence of the "new breed" of songwriters in country music whose directness and sincerity "opened up new realms of expression for country singers and writers" (Malone and Neal, 305). In a time of simple rhymes and premises, the more complex lyrics of a group of new songwriters had flourished: John Hartford's flowing, interior monologues; Chris Gantry's complex characterizations; Tom T. Hall's intricate storytelling; Shel Silverstein's whimsical, yet versatile lyrics; Jimmy Webb's structurally sophisticated lyrics; Mickey Newbury's psychological musings, and Kristofferson's visceral, passionate lyrics. Other songwriters who have continued to follow in the footsteps of these innovative songwriters named above are Guy Clark, Rodney Crowell, and John Prine. The new freedom of expression contributed to country music's opportunities for black, Hispanic, and Jewish singer-songwriters, and, most importantly, the large number of women who became superstars. These developments facilitated the "departures from the traditional norm . . . of a music dominated by adult male white Protestants" (Malone and Neal, 306).

The brilliance of Kristofferson's lyrics had attracted even more artists and producers who wanted to record the songs; and since almost everyone complained about his voice, established singers were the first to record the songs. And while money was never a motivation for creativity for Kristofferson, at this time he rejoiced in Roger Miller's cover and paid his son's medical bills. Other singers of note to record his songs were Willie Nelson, Bobby Bare, Tony Martin, Dean Martin, Andy Williams, Loretta Lynn, Gladys Knight, Patti Page, Engelbert Humperdinck, Chet Atkins, Al Green, O. C. Smith, Tompall Glaser, Marilyn Sellars, and Brenda Lee. The number of artists who have recorded his songs is somewhere near five hundred. Kristofferson's own voice, not tolerated in recordings before Fred Foster had been struck by his manner of delivery, doomed his first album, *Kristofferson*. Universal scorn for his voice limited sales to a paltry thirty thousand copies, even as audiences and musicians clamored for more of his songs.

At about the same time the album was released, Kristofferson's "For the Good Times" was recorded by popular country-pop artist Ray Price, whose elegant voice introduced Kristofferson's creative excellence to a huge chunk of the musical public. Price's recording, suggesting the ease with which the song might fit into the popular music category, embraces the pulsing country-rhythm signatures but features strings that, while unusual in country music, add unforeseen dimensions to the song. They enhance the complex relationship between the pair, suggesting alternative readings of the situation depicted, and foreshadow the loneliness ahead. A painful yet eloquent depiction of the end of a relationship, "For the Good Times" was named Song of the Year for 1970 by the Academy of Country Music. A few months later, Johnny Cash released a cover of "Sunday Morning Coming Down"—Kristofferson insisted Cash was the perfect singer with the perfect voice for this song—whose success was so complete that the Country Music Association (CMA) bestowed upon it the Song of the Year Award for 1970, winning for Kristofferson the same award from country's two rival organizations for the same year with different songs. When he won the CMA award for "Sunday Morning Coming Down," he was stunned. A famous video shows Roy Clark presenting the award to a dazed and emotional Kristofferson, who some critics claimed was stoned. Having been seated at the rear of the auditorium with no knowledge of the way to the stage, he took some time to find it. When he came into view, the audience was shocked at his disheveled appearance; he wore a crumpled suede jacket with no tie and sported long, unkempt hair. In a roomful of tuxedos, Kristofferson's manner of dress was seen as a gesture of disrespect, and the traditionalists were outraged. At the podium, he murmured his gratitude to Johnny Cash, and to quote Bill Malone, the award marked "the high point of his career and a . . . turning point in country music" (306). Additionally, he was named Songwriter of the Year (1970) by the Nashville Songwriters Association, an award acknowledging his entire output that year. Kristofferson said, "The people tied up with CMA and the Opry are the conservative element and it surprised me the most when I found that people were upset with my appearance, because most were friends I'd worked with for years before and they knew me" (Rensin, 29).

Ironically, the song awarded the CMA Single of the Year in 1970 was Merle Haggard's "Okie from Muskogie," a song that appears to target the counterculture for which Kristofferson had become an icon. The award for Album of the Year went to Haggard's *Okie from Muskogie*; Haggard himself won both the CMA male vocalist and the CMA entertainer of the year awards. A 2005 *GQ* interview with Haggard, however, indicates he regretted the song very soon after recording it because it drew undesirable attention (Heath).

Kristofferson's first LP, *Kristofferson* (1970), was given a rousing welcome by *Rolling Stone*. Ray Rezos saw it as a "superb album," in which Kristofferson "sings simple songs that speak eloquently of his experiences." He found Kristofferson to be a "remarkably strong and expressive singer" and also thought a "lot of the credit for the success of this album obviously goes to Fred Foster, whose relationship goes deeper than business" (38). While other reviewers were far less considerate of Kristofferson's voice, a great majority heaped praise upon his lyrics.

As one might expect, the songs in Kristofferson's first album define a historical and countercultural moment in time. Dominated by the idea of personal freedom, these songs also radiate beams that illuminate alienation, loneliness, honesty, and intimacy; and since his always-confessional songs first issued forth during the most emotionally transformative state of his life, at least to that point, his emphasis on freedom of expression is no less important. "Every album that I've cut, going back to the first one, has been . . . a reflection of what I'm going through at the time," he has said (Thibodeaux, C2).

Arguably his most famous song, "Me and Bobby McGee," which demonstrates his view of freedom, was written atop an oil rig during one of his trips to Louisiana. "I've always loved the feeling of Louisiana," Kristofferson said. "It just had a soul . . . that was different from any place in the United States. There was something about it that just appealed to me the same way that a lot of Europe does" (Thibodeaux, C2). The song describes a nomadic couple hitchhiking across the country—first introduced thumbing a ride from Baton Rouge to New Orleans and typical of the vast number of countercultural young, rootless people in the 1960s. The couple becomes separated near Salinas, California, but the speaker grieves deeply for his partner. Fred Foster, credited with coauthorship of this song, provided Kristofferson with the name of the secretary (Bobby McKee) for noted songwriter Boudleaux Bryant, convinced that the girl's name would be perfect song material. However, Kristofferson misunderstood the last name, thinking it was McGee; he was also offended by Foster's action, growling, "I don't write on assignment," but nevertheless felt obligated to follow his boss's advice. Several months later, he completed the song. He had recently seen Federico Fellini's *La Strada* (1954) and was deeply affected by the Italian director's film. The film follows the story of a simple-minded girl who was sold by her mother to a brutal circus performer, who after a time left her on a road while she was asleep. He later heard the same song the girl sang frequently, being sung by a woman who told him the girl had died. The film ends with the man on a beach howling at the stars in his grief. In an online interview, Kristofferson stated the man "was free when he left the girl, but it destroyed him . . . and that was the feeling at the end of 'Bobby McGee'" (Hutchinson, "Kristofferson's 'Me and Bobby McGee'"). The song's speaker laments he "let her slip away"; he cries, "I'd trade all of my tomorrows for a single yesterday," and remembers "holding Bobby's body next to mine." This view of freedom is frequently spoken of by Kristofferson, as "the burden of freedom," the title of a song he wrote in 1967 and included in his third album, *Border Lord* (1972).

Another early song wherein the pursuit of freedom has resulted in dismal consequences is "Sunday Morning Coming Down," the CMA winner for 1970. The song details the misery of a hangover. It notes the speaker's headache and uncertain stomach, unclean face, and tangled hair that trouble him after he awakens; he puts on his "cleanest dirty shirt" and prepares to "meet the day." The somewhat wry tone disappears in the second verse as the speaker goes outside and is overcome by a Proustian onslaught of buried memories activated by his senses: in the park, he sees children playing (one with her daddy); crossing the street, he encounters the "Sunday smell of someone frying chicken"; passing by a church, he hears voices singing; and, farther up the "Sunday morning sidewalk," he hears a "lonely bell" ringing, echoing his "disappearing dreams of yesterday." Aching with loneliness and alienation, the speaker renders a powerful evocation of alcoholism and the loss of traditional values (family, home, and faith)—not unlike Kristofferson's own situation—and the burden of freedom that follows that loss.

Also from the first album, "Help Me Make It through the Night," also written atop an oil rig in Louisiana, went on to win the Country Music Association's Single of the Year in 1971. The idea for it may well have come from Kristofferson's having listened to Bob Dylan's "I'll Be Your Baby Tonight" a great many times, as that was one of his favorite Dylan songs at that time. Heavily criticized on Music Row for its open sexuality, the song attracted the attention of numerous musicians, who, struck by Kristofferson's frank depiction of loneliness, wanted to cover it. Surprisingly, Sammi Smith's version of the song followed several others, all reflecting the male viewpoint, because it was written from Kristofferson's viewpoint. By changing the opening line from "Take the ribbon from your hair" to "Take the ribbon from my hair," Smith identifies herself as a seductress, a fact that some audiences found insufferable. Her version was chosen number 1 in *Heartaches by the Number: Country Music's 500 Greatest Singles*, by David Cantwell and Bill Friskics-Warren, who named it so because it was a huge crossover smash that "signaled country's belated arrival in the rock and soul era"; also accounting for its status were the lyrics of Kristofferson, who "takes the period's political and cultural impulses—impulses endemic to, among others, the civil rights, women's, and counterculture movements—and boils them down to their emotional essence: the desire for community, freedom, and love, and the suffering that results when those needs go unmet" (1–2). The song's production emphasizes Smith's husky-voiced delivery of Kristofferson's appeal for a brief human connection in a cold world.

Kristofferson's "For the Good Times," recorded by Ray Price, had a difficult time being recorded. Because it clearly refers to a sexual situation, its first recording by Bill Nash received very little radio play; moreover, Kristofferson discovered it was not easy to find any artists willing to record the song. The song was written in a flash of inspiration on one of his trips to Louisiana and then onto the offshore oil rigs in the Gulf of Mexico. He remembered,

> [On] one of those drives from Nashville to the Gulf I began a song about making love to a woman for the last time. After a while the melody really got to me. I couldn't wait to get to a guitar. I was riding along thinking of that part where it says, "Hear the whisper of the raindrops blowing soft against the window," and I wondered what the chords were. I wondered if I could play it. I wrote only the first

part of the lyrics then. A while went by before I finished it; I can't remember how long . . . but I do remember who I wrote it about. (Miller, 79)

Kristofferson's first track fires a salvo at conservative hypocrisy—certainly not the recommended way to introduce a country music album—but one that gives every implication that the album's attack on hypocrisy has just begun. "Blame It on the Stones" tosses a mocking jibe at middle-class morality, with more than a bit of a swipe at Kristofferson's mother's disdain for his chosen life's endeavor. The song depicts various archetypes of conservative dissemblers who affect piousness yet follow a less-than-righteous path themselves: Mr. Marvin Middleclass sips martinis and wonders "what the younger generation's coming to"; mother complains to the bridge club (Kristofferson's mother and wife were avid bridge players) about the rising cost of tranquilizers (a reference to the Rolling Stones' "Mother's Little Helper"); and father's late nights at work are spent pursuing his secretary, despite his concern for broken homes. The Salvation Army–style chorus, sarcastically singing "Bringing in the Sheaves," a well-known hymn, calls for the audience to join together in condemning the Rolling Stones for corruption, drug, and alcohol abuse.

Kristofferson's impulse toward creative freedom quite naturally examines the sphere of law and order, as he had occasionally taken the wrong path in that area himself. "The Best of All Possible Worlds," giving a weighty nod to Voltaire's *Candide*, a satire criticizing the optimistic view of numerous Enlightenment thinkers, relates a true story in which Kristofferson spoke disrespectfully to a police officer and paid the price. In these long, poetic lines frequently found in his early works, the song caustically describes his brutal treatment by the police, resulting from his observation, made while drunk, that the black and poor were routinely abused. However, the record company objected to his phrase "black or poor as me" and replaced it, over his protests, with "low-down poor as me." "The Law Is for the Protection of the People" is a sharp antiestablishment commentary on targeting anyone who is different from those around one (in this case, hippies); the commentary is carried out while hypothetically serving the public good. The song sarcastically provides three vignettes illustrating authorities bent on "protecting decent folks like you and me": police officers throw a man

in jail who merely stumbles and falls; redneck cops hold down an innocent hippie and cut his hair, announcing, "We don't need no hairy-
headed hippies scaring decent folks like you and me"; and officials hang
an innocent Jesus on the cross, proclaiming, "We don't need no riddle-
speaking prophets scaring decent folks like you and me (yes sirree)."

If, in writing songs reflecting his psychological and emotional
circumstance at any given time, Kristofferson has written the song of
himself, it follows that "To Beat the Devil" occupies a unique spot in his
musical canon and his life. The song begins with a spoken narration that
describes the desperate situation the speaker finds himself in. It's win-
tertime, and he is cold, hungry, and without money; but his hunger runs
deeper than his famishment for food. He retreats into a tavern whose
"friendly shadows" hint of losing himself there, but he has more reason
to fear from his direct encounter with the devil himself. In the form of
an old man, the devil puts the narrator to a severe test. Bill Friskics-
Warren sees the narrator as "an archetypal Kristoffersonian troubadour
trying to find himself" (1), by seeking out the hazardous murky territories in an effort to encourage self-discovery. Whether seeking darkness
is the work of the devil or the narrator, the darkness offers the narrator
despair, as well as an opportunity for transformation. Other narrators of
songs in this first album, namely Billy Dee and Casey, engage their dark
sides "to satisfy a thirst [they] couldn't name" and come to tragic ends.
The danger is heightened by the devil's smirk at the narrator's gnawing
hunger; the devil taunts the narrator and his lack of success, and sings a
song advising him that his efforts toward communicating his feelings
through songs are futile because "no one wants to know." "You know,"
the speaker responds, "the devil haunts a hungry man," and resolves to
continue in his quest, saying, "I've got to feed the hunger in my soul."
The speaker/narrator concedes that while he may not have won the
contest with the devil, "I drank his beer and then I stole his song." The
speaker's confession, "I was born a lonely singer and I'm bound to die
the same," while enunciating Kristofferson's persona of the solitary
singer fighting off despair, leads into a refusal to give up, with the
resounding line, "I don't believe that no one wants to know." Inciden-
tally, about thirty-seven years later, Kristofferson was asked if there
were times when he thought the devil was right, and it was true that no
one wants to know. He responded, "There were many times, when I'd
get to the last line and sing, 'I don't believe that no one wants to know,'

but I was thinking, 'Well, I've had a lot of people that didn't want to know'" (Cooper, 5).

Kristofferson's blending of poetic storytelling with his narrative songs has made them favorites with much of his musical audience. *Kristofferson* includes three songs about characters outside society's mainstream: "Casey's Last Ride," "Darby's Castle," and "Duvalier's Dream," all bearing upon loneliness and alienation. One of Kristofferson's grittier songs, "Casey's Last Ride" focuses on Casey, whose fate, as indicated by the heavy licks on the guitar and the dominant bass, is a hellish existence underground, possibly from substance abuse. While underground, Casey "ignores the fatal echoes of the clicking of the turnstiles and the rattle of his chains"; and, removed from anything natural, such as sunshine or rain, the air he breathes is poisonous. To fight the chill in his bones, he visits a bar and "drinks his pint of bitter," taking no notice of anyone around him. In the song's bridge are two alternate verses, presumably once spoken to Casey by his former love, but that now appear in the song only as his memories. In the two verses, the melody shifts from the minor key of the primary narrative, forsaking the heavy guitar and bass for violins that back her tender line, "It's so blessed good to feel your body." After her last line, "Casey, it's a shame to be alone," the violins play briefly and end the song on a melancholy note. In Kristofferson's album, the song is striking in its somewhat dynamic production amid the plainer use of instrumentation for the other songs.

"Darby's Castle" tells of Cecil Darby, a man obsessed with providing his wife with material possessions, specifically a huge house on top of a hill. Thinking only of rooms for the house, he neglects his wife, never seeming to hear her cry. One night he hears a sound in her room and, upon rushing in, discovers in the moonlight that "two bodies lay entangled" on the bed. As in many of his songs, Kristofferson notes the damage done to lonely and isolated individuals who are denied human contact, in this case brought on by the husband's misplaced priorities in his marriage. The brokenhearted husband then burns down the house, which "took three hundred days for the timbers to be raised" but is brought down in one night. Ironically, the three hundred days perhaps do not fully represent he amount of time that the wife had been neglected by her husband in his enthusiasm for things at the expense of companionship and intimacy. In "Duvalier's Dream," the main character is a lonely, disillusioned man who has "shunned the world of mortals." Duvalier mistrusts humanity in general and avoids close association with other people. The refrain goes, "It's hard to keep believing when you know you've been deceived." Duvalier meets a woman, whose "burning beauty cut him like a knife." Her sensuous beauty was not to be resisted, and "she smiling stepped aside to watch him fall." Duvalier, "betrayed by his own body and the hunger in his soul," returned to being an embittered dreamer.

Kristofferson has said, "The reason I came to Nashville was that the lyrics here were the best that I could identify from my experience. The people that were writing the closest thing to white man's soul music were country writers. They were writing about real life. . . . I figured the most honest you could be would be the most successful" (Price, 4).

3

"HAD TO TRY TO SATISFY A THIRST HE COULDN'T NAME"

1971–1975

At the beginning of 1971, life for Kris Kristofferson was a flurry of excitement. He and his band were entangled in an seemingly endless blur of clubs, stages, hotels, and cities. "It was like I had stepped onto a train or something and it was going. And I was just going along, trying to stay ahead of it . . . trying to put together music that made sense and just keep doing what I was doing," he said (Streissguth, 89). Despite his maddening schedule, life was easier for him than in the past; he had money coming in, and he could carouse between shows.

But not surprisingly, performing was not as pleasurable as it should have been at that point. His old foe, stage fright, had never been vanquished, and Kristofferson, an introvert, found performing a frightening activity. The debilitating feeling of being naked before an audience, especially when performing his own songs, had made drinking necessary for him to continue. But the drinking accelerated in both amount and opportunity, resulting in his being drunk through every performance and causing him to behave badly and frequently view the audience as the enemy. Once while in kindergarten back in Brownsville, he was asked to sing a song during a school play; when the time came, he turned his back to the audience and sang to the wall. His mother was horrified at his behavior, but the incident indicated the extreme stage fright he fought his entire life.

During his frenetic eighteen-month touring schedule, Kristofferson was ragged from alcohol consumption and walking pneumonia. His guitarist, Stephen Bruton, placed the blame for Kristofferson's condition on their grueling pace. "It just did not stop," he said. "You'd be . . . two pages from the end of your itinerary, and you'd get another itinerary" (Eals, 211–12). Kristofferson said he was "really in rough shape. We had been working forever. As tired and hung over and sick as I was, I'd . . . barely make it" (Eals, 212). His performances also told a story: he stared at the floor and frequently turned his back on the audience all the while mumbling his song lyrics in a jagged frog-like voice. British actress Samantha Eggar, his companion who attended some of his shows in Chicago in May 1971, observed, "Kris was very uncomfortable. He found it difficult to face the audience, even at the end of his songs. His songs were so brilliant, but I don't think people even got them at that time" (Eals, 212). Eventually, in 1971, he was hospitalized for a week, during which time he allowed his beard to grow freely. Critics claimed it was a calculated declaration of nonconformity; his fans, however, saw it was the new face of country music.

During the same year, Kristofferson was at work at Monument recording *The Silver Tongued Devil and I*, one of the most anticipated of all his albums. Four songs written by him had already scaled the charts, achieving success for the artists who had recorded them, but he had yet to be recognized as a recording artist. It was hoped by Kristofferson and Fred Foster that his second album might accomplish that transition. The album's songwriting itself, while not poised to surpass the excellence of the first album, having evolved over a much longer period of time, is still a striking example of his enormous creative talent. Two of the songs had been previously recorded by other artists and were now being offered for the first time by Kristofferson. The production of the album was also somewhat elevated, featuring violins in three of the songs and a horns section in another, ironically moving the music away from country toward the mainstream.

The front of the album displays a picture of Kristofferson standing and facing the camera steadfastly, while to his right and behind his body exists a fainter representation of him that projects a shadowy image of the silver-tongued devil. The album sleeve note written by Kristofferson requests prospective listeners to "call these echoes of the going-ups and coming-downs, walking pneumonia and run of the mill madness colored with guilt, pride, and a vague sense of despair."

The title track, "The Silver Tongued Devil and I," invites his audience once again to contemplate the devil, one of his most enduring subjects—which, together with despair, loneliness, and alienation, is interwoven throughout his lyrics as a source of his soul's undying torment. The song begins with the speaker's visit to the Tally-Ho Tavern, a popular establishment near Music Row in Nashville. (A favorite with musicians, the Tally-Ho, where Kristofferson once worked as a bartender in the 1960s, no longer exists, having been demolished for the sake of progress.) He enters and sits down beside a "tender young maiden"; and while he searches "from bottle to bottle" for a way to begin an "unfoolish" conversation, "that silver tongued devil just slipped from the shadows" and spirited her away. The speaker warned her of the devil who hides his evil intentions; it turns out she was aware of his lies but could not be persuaded otherwise. The silver-tongued devil, who dwells in the shadow, or the darker side of the speaker's existence, is a potent, assertive intruder into his negotiations with females; having "nothing to lose," he frequently directs the speaker, particularly under the influence of alcohol, toward actions he might not normally take. The speaker laments the inclinations of a woman to "offer her charms to the darkness and danger" and respond to a stranger "who'll love her and leave her alone." In this song and "The Taker," previously recorded by Waylon Jennings, Kristofferson speaks out about men's treatment of women and the willingness of some women to invite men to treat them badly. "The Taker" describes a man who gives a woman attention, opens doors to new places and experiences, and gets her into a world she has hungered for; he does this "because he's a taker," who will take her places, "take his time before taking advantage," and after he takes the "body and soul" that she offers him, "he'll take her for granted," and then "he'll take off and leave her." Kristofferson was very attractive to women; in fact, Canadian singer Ronnie Hawkins, also contracted to Monument, said of him, "He was a lady's man beyond belief . . . women made fools of themselves around Kris" (quoted in Miller, 120a). As this song, like his others, reflects his own state of mind at the time he wrote the song, Kristofferson likely suffered from guilt regarding his own deception of women by way of his own silver tongue; and notwithstanding his delight in the charms of women, he quite possibly cringed at their display of lack of self-respect.

From these musings upon the male-female conundrum, Kristofferson's album goes on to include two intimate love songs, two story songs, and one of his most famous songs, "The Pilgrim, Chapter 33." His introduction cites a list of musicians who provided inspiration for the song that, conceived by Kristofferson, also appears to be a sharply introspective look at himself at the age of thirty-three, while he was still endeavoring to become a successful songwriter in Nashville. The pilgrim, a wasted person who wears "yesterday's misfortunes like a smile," is bereft of "money, love and dreams." He has lost "all he's loved along the way," but he continues to search for a place of success and respect. Images of futility pervade, giving off more than a "vague sense of despair," as he is far from home and wondering if believing in himself is "a blessing or a curse." He is also plagued by his own demons and his own innate oppositions and boundaries that prove him to be a "walking contradiction, partly truth and partly fiction," and cause him to "take every wrong direction on his lonely way back home." The despair is nevertheless countered by the insistence that "from the rocking of the cradle to the rolling of the hearse / The going up was worth the coming down." The depiction of a songwriter who struggles to survive the inherent pitfalls as he searches for the peace he has yet to find has become archetypal; yet, the self-destructive pilgrim seems to fit in with Kristofferson's preoccupation with the contradictory boundaries he first encountered early in his life.

Of the two story songs, "Jody and the Kid" has been recorded by various artists and remains quite popular. It was first recorded in 1968 by Roy Drusky, who achieved considerable success with it; ironically, it received significant playing time on the radio while Kristofferson was janitor at Columbia Recording Studios. The song's speaker tells of a little girl who became attached to him and attracted the attention of people in the community who would say, "There goes Jody and the kid." The girl waited for him every day and followed him to the river. They grew older, and still together, they became lovers. In the third verse, when "the world's a little older, and the years have changed the river," the speaker still walks the pathway to the levee "with another little girl who follows me." He remarks how the old folks smile to see her follow beside him, "doing little things the way her Mamma did," and how lonesome it gets when he hears someone saying, "There goes Jody and the kid."

The second story song, "Billy Dee," another instance of Kristofferson's sympathy with characters on the outskirts of society, surprises listeners with its first line: "Billy Dee was seventeen when he turned twenty-one." Dee, much like Kristofferson himself, "had to try to satisfy a thirst he couldn't name" and was inclined toward "getting high on women, words and wine." Self-destructive, Dee "took a beating from a world he meant no harm" in his efforts to go his way alone. He was discovered on the floor of his hotel, "reaching for the needle, Lord, that drove him down to hell."

Also appearing in this second album is "Breakdown (A Long Way from Home)," one of Kristofferson's songs from *Cisco Pike*, starring Gene Hackman as a crooked cop mixed up with drug dealing and Kristofferson playing an ex-rock star being blackmailed by the cop. Essentially referring to his wretched predicament in the film, the song also rings true concerning his own situation—his loneliness and great distance from home. The song depicts late night on a forsaken street, with nowhere to go and no one he knows. In his typical wordplay, Kristofferson sings, "So it's so long so many so far behind you," referring to friends he once had, and continues singing, "You still got the same lonely songs to remind you / Of someone you seemed to be, so long ago." He thinks to himself how he has come "All alone all the way / On your own"; then wonders, "Who's to say / That you've thrown it away for a song"; and finally muses, "Boy, you've sure come a long way from home."

In his second album and also in *Cisco Pike* is "Loving Her Was Easier (Than Anything I'll Ever Do Again)," Kristofferson's tender, intimate song dating back to 1969 when he accompanied Dennis Hopper to Peru for the filming of Hopper's infamous film, *The Last Movie*. Incorporating the picturesque landscape near the filming location into the striking imagery in the song's long, "perfectly metrical" poetic lines became one of the more notable aspects of an extraordinary song. "I have seen the morning burning golden on the mountain in the skies" begins a sublime introduction to the morning sun and the person lying beside the speaker as healers of his spiritless state. "The feeling of her fingers on my skin" wiped away the yesterdays and promised of tomorrows and the "money, love and time we had to spend." The closeness he felt with her he had never known, and he never knew "the answer to the easy way she opened every door in [his] mind." It was easy to believe it was never going to end, and "loving her was easier than anything I'll ever do again." Dave Hickey insists that "Loving Her Was Easier" and "Breakdown" are definitive Kristofferson cuts, insofar as they show what he "does best," and asserts that "any of the instruments can do what they want to, to give the song some *kick*, as long as one rhythm instrument supports the melody structure" (30).

The album includes "Good Christian Soldier," written by Billy Joe Shaver and Bobby Bare, about a preacher's son who, as a child, prayed nightly to grow up to become a good Christian soldier. Many years later, in Vietnam, the same young man prayed not to be a good soldier but "to make it through another day." The song contends that "it's hard to be a Christian soldier when you tote a gun," and goes on to say, "It's getting hard to tell what's wrong from right," echoing the general post-Vietnam stance.

The tribute to Janis Joplin, "Epitaph (Black and Blue)," was written by Kristofferson and Donnie Fritts. Fritts tells the story of Kristofferson's hearing Joplin's posthumously released album, *Pearl*, for the first time:

> He listened to it over and over again because he felt like this was going to be a real big record, you know. He was going to be hearing it, and he wanted to get used to hearing it just by himself. Well, we wrote a song with her in mind that night. "Why was she born so black and blue" is how we started. . . . When we wrote the song, I did it with just very simple chord changes. But when I got home, I added all these R&B passing chords. It would not change the melody, but it would just put it a little bit somewhere else.
>
> The next morning we were in the studio, and I got Kris over to this piano. . . . And I showed him what I had done. Well, I didn't know Fred Foster was in the control room. He said, "That is what I want to hear on this record, exactly the way you did it. I don't want anything else on the record. I just want you two." Later on, I think they put strings on the last verse. (Streissguth, 88–89).

Critic Dave Hickey's esteem for the album seems vaguely unsettling: "There has never been and probably never will be a better songwriter album; I don't see how Kristofferson is ever going to write a better batch of songs; the material will create such demands on him that he will never have the peace to write again. From now on it will be band writing and studio writing" (30).

Heading to Nashville in November 1971 for a cover story for *Life* magazine, Kristofferson met Rita Coolidge while she was waiting to board the flight to Memphis to rehearse with her band, the Dixie Flyers, before going on tour. They sat together on the trip from Los Angeles and discovered the existence of a strong mutual attraction between them. He disembarked with her in Memphis, ignoring his scheduled interview in Nashville. Not just an attractive female ripe for a brief relationship, Coolidge and he connected very quickly on a deep level, seeming to Kristofferson as if he was coming home.

A graduate of Florida State University, Coolidge had majored in art but later realized she would rather sing than teach art. Coming from a family that loved music, she and her sisters had performed as the Coolidge Sisters before she went to college, and she had relied on her singing to help out financially during college. After graduation, she moved to Memphis and sang jingles for Pepper-Tanner, Memphis's biggest jingle factory, with her sight-reading getting her studio work; at Pepper-Tanner, she was allowed to record a single, "Turn Around and Love You," a surprise hit in Los Angeles when she arrived there. She began singing backing vocals for the group, Delaney & Bonnie and Friends, touring in late 1969 with Eric Clapton and George Harrison, and was also a featured soloist with Joe Cocker's Mad Dogs and Englishmen troupe that included Leon Russell. At the end of the tour, she was singing on albums with Stephen Stills, Eric Clapton, Dave Mason, and other artists. Her unique voice and artistic style earned her a recording contract with A&M Records; her first album, an eponymously titled album, incorporated the talents of many of the musicians she had recently worked with. The exotic Coolidge, of Cherokee and Scottish ancestry, had grown up loving soul, rhythm, and blues music, and says that while recording the album, she felt she was searching for the style she was meant to be doing. Finding her strength lay in ballads and songs, she persisted in her artistic refinement, carefully choosing material that would allow her to "touch people's hearts" (Crowe).

While each initially attempted to pursue a solitary schedule and meet up frequently, the frantic pace soon became absurd, and she and Kristofferson united both their professional and personal lives. "Besides being two people in love," Coolidge observed, it was a "mutual marriage too" (Crowe). Kristofferson immediately introduced her on his live shows, and she appeared with him on tour and as backup and guest singer on his albums. Although she chafed under the Country Queen title she acquired when she paired up with Kristofferson, the benefits of the addition of her voice to his are apparent instantly; her clear, pure voice seems to smooth out his rough edges, making the harmony strong and captivating. And although he was clearly the star whenever they appeared together, she was always quite gracious, finding time all the while to keep her own career moving forward. When she and Kristofferson were married, she had recorded three albums, *Rita Coolidge* and *Nice Feeling*, both released in 1971, and *The Lady's Not for Sale*, in 1972, which featured songs by songwriters including Stephen Stills, Graham Nash, Leon Russell, Neil Young, and Bob Dylan.

In the continued fulfillment of Kristofferson's contract with Monument, his third album, *Border Lord* (1972), was expected to secure his success as a recording artist and dispel any doubts about his ability to generate songs and record them at a rate and quality to sustain an appreciative audience. Kristofferson's liner notes declare, "We put a lot of road between this album and the last one, back and forth across the U.S. of A. and Canada, hitting most of the high spots and all of the lows. Cruising pretty close to crazy but somehow keeping it together enough to keep from crossing that border." An album of original compositions, *Border Lord* seems to have benefited from earlier compositions, some with dates of 1967 and 1968 that imply origins from his time with Marijohn Wilkin and Buckhorn Music. While this album inspired interest in Kristofferson as an outlaw bent on crossing borders and breaking rules, the liner notes suggested the songs might well furnish an account of his life on the road. However, only three songs seem related specifically to touring, and they refer to activities that had come to define his life. The title song, "Border Lord," employing Kristofferson's characteristic wordplay, recounts leaving Minnesota early one rainy morning with hungover band members "a-humming to a half forgotten echo" and "thinking of the time we never had the time to take." A lone guitar begins the song, gradually increases to full band strength, utilizes major/minor key shifts throughout, and with the various instruments eventually falling away, leaves at the end the lone guitar—all providing an impressive background for a song whose key lines are, "When you're heading for the border lord / You're bound to cross the line." The territories of convention and commitment are certainly implied through the sense of defiance and rebellion: certain lines run like anthems through the song: "Breaking any ties before they bind you" and "Running like you're running out of time" infer a need to reject commitment and maintain personal freedom at all costs. "Take it all—take it easy—till it's over" shows the effects of Kristofferson's own personal demons on conventional concepts of personal obligations.

"Getting By High and Strange" pays tribute to life on the road and enjoying drugs and one-night stands; the song salutes a self-destructive existence and celebrates the freedom to pursue that existence. "Burden of Freedom" meditates upon Kristofferson's concern with the consequences of his insistence on personal freedom. In the song, he details the responses of people, presumably family members, who are angry and frustrated with his behavior. He describes himself standing on the stairway leading out of the dungeon, with freedom quite close at hand; he is damned by those behind him "for seeking salvation / they don't understand." He asks for the Lord's help in shouldering the burden of freedom and for the courage "to be what I can." He then describes the "lonely frustration" of those who erupt in derisive laughter because he demands the freedom to travel "where no one can follow." He asks for the Lord's help in forgiving those who "don't understand," but at the end of the song, when he thinks of having wounded "the last one who loved me," he asks the Lord to help her to forgive him, saying, "I don't understand."

Part William Blake, whose pronouncement concerning the duty and obligation of every artist to develop his talent had become the primary force in his life, and part result of his disownment by his family, his mandate to live an artist's life as he thought it should be lived hinged on the concept of personal freedom. Besides requiring the independence to function as a singer-songwriter, he chose several maxims from Blake's writings to use as specific guides in his life and career. One of his favorites, "The road to excess leads to the palace of wisdom," could be seen to advocate a life of drugs, alcohol, and women, at least for a touring musician in the early 1970s. All this was influenced by the self-destructive appeal of "live fast and die young" in the manner of Hank Williams, or the ravaged Johnny Cash—whose glittering image at Ryman Auditorium that fateful day in May of '65 had persuaded Kristofferson to throw himself into songwriting and set about to emulate Cash. Dennis Hopper, friend of Kristofferson, and cowriter, director, and costar of *Easy Rider* (1969), the generation-defining film of the counterculture sixties, has spoken of the lure of self-destruction, observing that the early 1960s marked the emergence from an era caught up with the idea of the artist as a tragic figure who had a "kind of passion" that made it necessary to suffer and produce tortured works, or become an alcoholic or drug addict, and die young (*Kris Kristofferson: His Life and Work*). But while Kristofferson's freedom allowed him to live as he thought an artist should live, the difficulties this conviction brought into his marriages were devastating. Following her divorce from him, Rita Coolidge lamented that even after "he got sober, he continued to have women, and it just broke my heart" (Earle). Looking back on their marriage of sixteen years (in 1999), his third wife, Lisa Meyers, recalls, "I was trying to raise babies and just have a normal life. . . . I spent the better part of two or three years trying to [tame him] and then, at the end of that time, I remember sitting there thinking, 'OK, he's nice looking, but I can't find one other thing I like about this man. Not one'" (Rose). "But, she stuck it out through some hard years," says Kristofferson. (In 2013, they celebrated thirty years of marriage.) He admits he "had a lot of bad habits [he] was very reluctant to get rid of" but acknowledges, "I had fought for my independence and had fought for my freedom to do as I believed I was supposed to; and, you know, I was wrong" (Rose).

Of the ten remaining songs in *Border Lord*, six concern people, mostly women, on the fringes of society. "Somebody Nobody Knows" depicts a young girl in a barroom and an old man in the gutter, each "just a soul in the shadows the world never sees." Both are in desperate situations—the girl smiles vacantly as she stares into the eyes of men, and the old man is in tears as he attempts to clean himself up—and each one is "dying alone." Kristofferson's lifelong affinity with those whom "the world threw away," heightened by Williams's songs and Blake's verses, is echoed here in songs that provide glimpses of women who move uncertainly through borders of various landscapes. "Josie" tells of the woman the speaker had idealized since before he left Texas, "even though [he] didn't know it at the time"; he says that "she was proud of her young body" and "she loved me back to living at a time I was lost," before she left on her way to burn bridges. He wonders if she's "grown harder than [her] years" while "selling . . . her sadness on the street" and asks, "How much did you lose between the laughter and the tears?" The speaker finds the road now is colder as he journeys from one empty place to another, and while he suspects she is not looking for him, he thinks someday he may "just chase her down again." Interestingly, Kristofferson's depiction of Josie as "Looking like a lonesome little girl," matches the speaker's feelings of loneliness, suggesting the source of her need to burn bridges and his prolonged journeying. "Little Girl Lost" also speaks of "the little girl" who once loved the speaker, but now "the devil's got her soul; and, in "When She's Wrong," the speaker gives a word of warning to his successor, trying to alert him to the devastating pain he will endure because of her. "Stagger Mountain Tragedy" relays the story of the speaker's journey down the mountain from the sunshine-covered top to the darkness where the girl who "danced to the tune the devil played" set the speaker's demons loose with her dancing, provoking him to kill her; the speaker in "Smokey Put the Sweat on Me" tells of meeting the "raven haired Cajun-looking devil" who captivates him, thus causing him to lose his freedom. Themes of traveling or journeying within borders, or the consequences of crossing them, play in counterpoint throughout *Border Lord.*

In March 1972, Kristofferson and Coolidge accepted an invitation from their friend, Willie Nelson, to the Dripping Springs Reunion Festival, a three-day country music festival, conceived as Austin's answer to Woodstock. It was designed by inexperienced promoters who insisted they could attract almost two hundred thousand visitors and counted on using Nelson's name to launch and maintain a huge annual event. Scheduled performers included noted country music artists Roger Miller, Loretta Lynn, Bill Monroe, Earl Scruggs, Roy Acuff, Buck Owens, Charlie Rich, and Hank Snow; and the scheduling of these country music icons alongside the younger songwriters that included Kristofferson and Lee Clayton acknowledged that the newcomers had been accepted in the country music world. Donnie Fritts, who attended this event with Coolidge and Kristofferson, said, "You'd look out there and it'd be hillbillies, cowboy guys, and then you have the hippies, all having fun together. I think that was a big part of what was developing there. . . . It was one of the most important gatherings of the seventies, bringing all the different acts and people together in one place. And it happened through Willie Nelson" (Streissguth, 135). The phenomenon

Fritts was describing taking place at Nelson's festival was the "official public coming-out" of progressive country (Flippo, "Country Music," 16), the country-rock fusion of the seventies, that after a lengthy gestation, had arrived. According to Chet Flippo, Nashville was undergoing encroachment by new and various record labels aimed at recording country and rock artists, and by the liberal wing of country and western. The origin of progressive country is still under question: numerous people in the seventies, including Kristofferson, Willie Nelson, and Tom T. Hall, have been named as stimulators, as well as earlier musicians, Johnny Cash, Earl Scruggs, and of course Hank Williams, who were contributors through their inclinations to reach out beyond the traditional country and western strictures and embrace the "liberal evolution." At Nelson's festival, Leon Russell, who sang early that morning, addressed the congregation that afternoon to say, "This is the greatest gathering of rednecks and hippies in history" (Flippo, "Country Music," 16). Flippo says Russell's comment is incorrect: "At least four fifths of the crowd of 35,000 was made up of long-hairs" (16). The event fell far below the number of expected fans and failed to make money. Nevertheless, the next year, Nelson was back with his expanding variety of fans for the beginning of his Fourth of July picnics that were wild affairs with the smorgasbord of fans and music styles that have become his trademark. Flippo continues, "The audience enjoyed twenty hours of excellent country music in a dust and sun bowl full of what one alarmed onlooker called 'heat-crazed, beer-sodden kids,' who were shedding their clothes along with their prejudices against country music" (16).

In November 1972, Monument Records released Kristofferson's fourth album, *Jesus Was a Capricorn*, a mere nine months after the third one. Critics were divided in their opinions of this album, with some more critical than others. The album was a runaway best seller thanks to the number 10 song on the album, which was originally released as a single. Following its release, "Why Me" was played repetitively by radio DJs, propelling it to number 1 on the country charts; Monument then rereleased the album to include the single, and it achieved gold status, becoming the most financially successful album Kristofferson ever recorded.

"Why Me" was originally thought to be a joke, especially by those who knew Kristofferson to be a well-educated intellectual whose leanings he himself has described as "left" of liberal. Soon his story behind the song began to circulate, and the song was understood to signify a true religious experience for Kristofferson. Later, he said, "It was just a personal thing I was going through at the time. I had some kind of experience that I can't even explain" (McClintock, 172–73). He recalls going with friends to a small fundamentalist church in Nashville, and during the service, listening to Larry Gatlin's song "Help Me (Lord)," also on *Jesus Was a Capricorn*, and being moved by it. He says that he had never thought of needing help, but he was feeling pretty low. The pastor, Jimmy Snow, singer Hank Snow's son, asked, "Is anybody feeling lost?" "Up goes my hand," Kristofferson says. Pastor Snow then asked, "Are you ready to accept Christ? Kneel down there." "I'm kneeling there," Kristofferson continues, "and I carry a big load of guilt around . . . and I was just out of control, crying. It was a release. It really shook me up" (McClintock, 173).

He appeared on WSM's *Friday Night Gospel Time* following the *Grand Ole Opry* show to an audience of two thousand people who heard him sing "Why Me," "Burden of Freedom," and "Pilgrim's Prayer," a duet with Larry Gatlin. He related the story behind the song, acknowledging that his performance then was his first completely sober one for a long time. He expressed hope that his religious experience might provide help with his drinking problem.

Despite the fact that Kristofferson's long-standing intellectual questionings and emotional torments would have likely not received much if any consideration from the prevailing religious current in Nashville, his song "Why Me" was received remarkably well. The forthright lyrics that issued a plea for salvation seemed to indicate to those in the country music realm he was possibly becoming a changed man.

Kristofferson took part in Explo '72, a weeklong festival in Dallas that drew over one hundred thousand followers from the United States and around seventy foreign countries. Sponsored by Campus Crusade for Christ, the event aspired to interest young people in careers in Christian service. Described by Billy Graham as "a religious Woodstock," the huge event promoted classes in Bible study by day, and by night everyone assembled for concerts. The final event, an eight-hour concert of preaching and music in the Cotton Bowl, was prominently attended by Graham, Johnny Cash, Children of the Day, Kristofferson, and Coolidge (Miller, 111).

Having declined other pleas for participation in connection with Explo '72, Kristofferson accepted Cash's offer to contribute to Cash's low-budget film about the life of Jesus to be filmed on location in Israel. For *The Gospel Road*, a labor of love by Cash, who personally financed the film, Kristofferson, Coolidge, and Larry Gatlin sang "Why Me," while Cash performed Kristofferson's song "Burden of Freedom."

In 1973, "Why Me" was awarded the Dove Award for the Gospel Song of the Year.

"Jesus Was a Capricorn," the title song for the album of the same name, depicts Jesus as the first hippie, wearing no shoes, eating organic foods, and believing in peace and love. The song quickly devolves into a discourse on intolerance, citing the hatred most people have for things they do not understand. Referring to racial prejudice, Kristofferson notes, "Everybody's got to have somebody to look down on." More than just a little personal venom is spewed in the direction of *Rolling Stone* reviewer Ben Gerson for his stinging barbs about his previous album. The second song, "Jesse Younger," seems to have been written with his family in mind, and specifically his continuing anger at their rejection. In it, Jesse is portrayed as a young man who "selfishly refused" to live his life the way his parents had planned, insisting on going his own way. Branded "a devil, not a man" for his treatment of his family, his estrangement from them means his "little baby brother is his father's and his mother's only son."

His two duets with Coolidge offer pleasant harmonies that look forward to *Full Moon*, their first duo album. "It Sure Was (Love)" and "Give It Time to Be Tender" highlight the extremes in their voices, but the elaborate instrumentation—piano, strings, and numerous guitars—indicates a soothing remove from Kristofferson's often gravelly song style. Their duets together seemed to betoken a commitment to overcome their essential differences and make every effort to produce harmonious music. "Nobody Wins" was recorded later by Brenda Lee, who with it secured a place for herself in country music. One of the more interesting songs on the album is "Sugar Man," about a junkie hooker who overdoses on heroin. Recalling the classic "The St. James Infirmary," the song's slow, bluesy account of the speaker's search for his "baby" he found "lying cold upon the bed" echoes Kristofferson's continuing preoccupation with women on the edge.

With the increase in albums and the popularity of his songs, Kristofferson found himself in greater demand for appearances. In 1972, he and his band, the Band of Thieves, consisting of Terry Paul on bass, Stephen Bruton on guitar, and Donnie Fritts on piano, performed in several cities in Europe and in London's prestigious Royal Albert Hall. While in the UK, Kristofferson and his band performed in Oxford, and he reunited with friends from his Rhodes scholarship days (Miller, 117). Back home in the United States, he fell into a succession of appearances on numerous television shows, usually with Coolidge. He was available for benefits and support of good causes, occasionally irritating more conservative members of the audience with his liberal views. He received awards from Broadcast Music Inc., sharing Songwriter of the Year in Country Music with writer and producer Billy Sherrill in 1971 and again in 1972, with five of his songs contributing to the award. Also in 1972, he shared the same award in the popular music category with Paul McCartney and George Harrison. In that same year, he received the Robert J. Burton Award for the most performed country song, "Help Me Make It through the Night"; he also appeared on *The David Frost Show* and was cited as Songwriter of the Year by the Nashville Songwriters Association.

On December 2, 1972, shortly after the release of *Jesus Was a Capricorn*, Kristofferson appeared in a concert performance, *Live at the Philharmonic*, at Philharmonic Hall in New York, at a significant point in his increasing popularity. The opening number was "The Late John Garfield Blues," written by John Prine, who was in the audience, along with Ronnie Hawkins and Ramblin' Jack Elliott. Kristofferson followed with several songs from his new album, all of which were unfamiliar to his audience. He then played one of his classics, "Loving Her Was Easier (Than Anything I'll Ever Do Again)," and a brand-new song, "Late Again (Getting Over You)," which would not be included on an album until *Spooky Lady's Sideshow* in 1974. At that point, he sang six songs from his earlier albums, finishing that group with a version of Merle Haggard's famous "Okie from Muskogie"; Kristofferson praised its author, his friend, but not the right-wing beliefs for which the song is famous. His surprise guest, at that time, was a little-known singer-songwriter named Willie Nelson, who was generously received and performed a four-song set. Kristofferson then introduced his "better half,"

Rita Coolidge, and another country musician moving quickly on his way toward success, Larry Gatlin.

In 1973, Paul Mazursky sought the services of Kristofferson in his film *Blume in Love*, one of his looks at modern marriage. He was also sought by Sam Peckinpah to play the part of Billy the Kid in a film that fought off delay after delay. Kristofferson and Coolidge finally succeeded in setting aside time for their marriage; the ceremony was held at her parents' house in Malibu and conducted by her father. Guests present included Fred Foster, James Coburn, Sam Peckinpah, the Coolidge family, friends, and musicians.

Kristofferson's and Coolidge's respective record companies—Monument and A&M—had agreed to a collaboration between the two, with A&M, her company, releasing the first album. Thereafter, the couple would record at alternate studios. One month following their wedding, their first album together, *Full Moon* (1973), was released. It contained primarily love song covers, with many being sung at a slow tempo to exhibit her silken voice. Keyed to her voice, the songs were intended to showcase her strengths, requiring Kristofferson to sing at a higher range than normal. Included were two songs composed by the couple jointly, and one older Kristofferson song, "From the Bottle to the Bottom," which won a Grammy for Best Country Vocal Performance by a Duo or a Group. His one new song, "A Song I'd Like to Sing," reached country and easy listening charts, as did their cover of Tom Jans's "Loving Arms." The album achieved gold certification.

Coolidge preferred not to live in Nashville, where Kristofferson had lived for eight years, but wanted a house in Malibu. Before long, she discovered she was pregnant; their daughter, Casey, was born in 1974. Coolidge took off six months after her child's birth, but Kristofferson continued his hectic pace. With no letup in the excesses connected with performing and touring, his alcohol consumption, drug intake, and cigarette habit all progressed at an alarming rate involving a staggering amount of toxic contaminants while his work pace never slowed. Not for want of money did Kristofferson work and "play" at such a manic pace, for he cared little for material possessions. But he forced himself mentally and physically to the point of collapse, his strenuous exertion appearing at times to be almost a desperate effort to rid himself of his demons. Once, during a stressful period, he spoke of the difficulty in maintaining perspective. He said, "I'd like not to be disappointed in myself and others. I get bitter. No matter how much you try it seems like people are only interested in their own bag. . . . Everybody wants a piece of you. Ultimately, they'd like to see you disembowel yourself onstage." But after seeming to weigh his comments, he said, "See there's the danger. Talking like that when most of them just come up and say you're great" (McClintock, 170). His schedule allowed no time for visiting with dear friends—he lamented in 1974 that he had not spoken with Johnny Cash in two years but was instead forced to spend time with people he did not like. His marriage never appeared to be idyllic, weighted down as it was with the pressures of his schedule and the tensions between his and Coolidge's careers (Burke, "Kristofferson's Talking Blues," 2:21–22).

One of the people whom he delighted in seeing was his old friend Marijohn Wilkin, who gave him his first job when he came to Nashville. Wilkin, having battled alcoholism herself, had reached an impasse in composing her song that was essentially the prayer of an alcoholic. She asked Kristofferson for help, and he helped her with a line, allowing the lines then to flow; to his surprise, she gave him cowriting credit for the song. Covered by many artists, "One Day at a Time" reflected the language of Alcoholics Anonymous meetings, originating in the early days of treatment centers and talking openly of alcoholism. It became a hit for Marilyn Sellars, Christy Lane, and Gloria Sherry in Ireland (Miller, 127–28).

Kristofferson also endeavored to help younger musicians struggling to break through. He met Steve Goodman, who opened for him at the Quiet Knight in Chicago, Goodman's hometown. Listening to Goodman sing, Kristofferson became speechless. Goodman sang "The City of New Orleans," his own song, and also "Sam Stone," a grim composition about an addicted war veteran—with the unforgettable line "There's a hole in daddy's arm where all the money goes"—written by his friend and Chicago mailman John Prine. Kristofferson arranged gigs for both of the young singers-songwriters at the Bitter End in New York, where he went following his stint in Chicago, and enlisted his friend, Canadian pop singer Paul Anka, in helping them secure recording contracts.

In 1974, Kristofferson's fifth album, *Spooky Lady's Sideshow*, was recorded at Hollywood's Sunset Sound studios, having moved from Fred Foster in Nashville to David Anderle and some exceptional studio musicians. Searching for the ultimate form of expression, Kristofferson saw this move as a step in that direction. "My limits are my own," he said to David Rensin. "The band can do anything I have the imagination to let them do—and they are stretching me, because I find things which used to be only in my imagination that I can do now" (32). Appearing about a year and a half after his previous album, *Spooky Lady's Sideshow* includes songs mostly written by Kristofferson, two of which he coauthored and one cover. The album has a new sound and, replete with variety, shows an impressive range hitherto unknown in his recordings. "Same Old Song" attempts to dispel any preconceptions about success, insisting that there is actually little difference between the bottom and the top, "just a few more friends that you'll be losing when you drop," and, while the nights are brighter, the bars are better and the sweet is sweeter, "them blues, well it's still the same old song." In fact, the songs that follow, although largely perceived to be concerned with excess to the point of dissipation, seem to represent a nightmarish vision of the underside of success. Mike Utley's rousing organ melodies in "Late Again" work in energies that are rare in Kristofferson's songs. The lyrics describe the miserable existence of the speaker who is permanently separated from his love. He drinks and he is lonely; he does not want conversation. In his aloneness, he seeks a relationship with a woman, saying, "Maybe I can learn to love her / While I'm a-getting over you." While the rollicking rhythm of this song belies the wretched condition of the speaker, another song, "I May Smoke Too Much," is a rowdy declaration of hedonism that seems close to a brawling, drinking song. "Now I love too much, fight too much," the speaker boasts in the song's chorus, "but you bet your butt I'm going to live before I die." The piano contributes its best honky-tonk as the speaker ends the song with the line "It's a low-down life, but it ain't gonna pass me by." Another song that depicts an opposite view of success is "Rock and Roll Time," in which the speaker is "falling behind" the normal pace of life because he's "running on rock and roll time." Some, he says, have called this procedure a crime and convicted those who have made it a practice. He details the trials of living in the normal world when one is accustomed to life on rock-and-roll time; he hopes heaven is happy and high and runs on "rock and roll time." In the chorus, the speaker calls out to be taken away to the "whiskey and wine / of some better day," as the backup singers slide into their harmonies a bit late to emphasize the point.

Into the album concerning the consequences of success is "From the Stairway to the Bottom," a strange, yet appropriate choice; it features the mirror acting as the speaker's conscience as he goes down the stairs to escape to pursue the wife of a friend. The process portrays him descending into the depths of human nature, as he lies to everyone he knows. Also presenting a hellish experience, "Shandy" details a woman who is apprehended crossing the border with illegal drugs and detained; Martin visits her bed and awakens drenched, screaming, and "dreaming of blood on the bed." The chorus repeats that "nightmares are somebody's daydreams," and "daydreams are somebody's lies." "One for the Money" is a song inspired by director Sam Peckinpah; "I've seen you standing there, stunned in the spotlight," says the speaker describing Peckinpah's struggles in making films. Also appropriate for the album that reflects hazards of success, its lines "'Cause you're easy to fool when you're lost in the stars / Shoot out that spotlight before you go blind" may be good advice to anyone who has become impressed with his or her own success. However, no album would be complete without a song about freedom, however ironic, and "Broken Freedom Song" continues in the vein of heartbreaking lyrics set to first-rate country-rock musical accompaniment. The "simple song of freedom" describes a soldier on a train "with his empty sleeve pinned to his shoulder," the result of fighting but not for freedom. Also pictured is a woman, pregnant, and waiting near a phone "for some man who never missed her"; she also waits by the door and "listens to the freedom / in the silence at her door." And lastly, the song speaks of a Savior who "wonders why His Father / left him bleeding and alone"; He hears the "broken song of freedom," in "a cross He never made," and "in a city full of strangers." The speaker closes saying, "Ain't no fun to sing this song no more."

But the next to last song on the album, "Smile at Me Again," begins with the speaker having a rough Monday morning and feeling as if he's losing his grip. "Nothing looks as empty / As a motel bed," he bemoans as he considers that he's "still a stranger / in this God-forsaken land." He plans to "take enough" to wake up and complete one last one-night stand, at which time he wants to go home to "something's going to smile at me again." He is ready to "break [his] connections," get rid of his equipment, and "let [his] friend, the Devil" be responsible for the rest. He will then head home to "something's / gonna smile at me again."

The final verse repeats the chorus in the album's first song, "Same Old Song," which reiterates that the nights, bars, and the sweet are all sweeter, but as for the blues, "it's still the same old song."

In late 1974, Kristofferson and Coolidge released their second duo album, *Breakaway*, recorded at Monument Records with Fred Foster, producer. Similar to the first album recorded at A&M, with her producer, David Anderle, who set the songs in Coolidge's keys, *Breakaway* also accommodated her voice, requiring Kristofferson to sing beyond his normal range, resulting in unanticipated harmony. Several songs were covers: "Lover Please," written by songwriter and musician Billy Swan and recorded by Clyde McPhatter in 1962, won a Grammy for the Best Country Vocal Performance by a Duo or a Group for 1975; the exquisite harmony on the ballad, "The Things I Might Have Been," written by Richard and Robert Sherman, added a new dimension to the famous solo song recorded by many different singers; Coolidge's and Kristofferson's duet of Melba Montgomery's song "We Must Have Been Out of Our Minds," recorded very successfully by Montgomery in a duet with George Jones back in 1963; and the couple's version of Larry Gatlin's "Rain," a song paying tribute to the large number of people who had died from drug overdoses, became quite popular. Kristofferson's two songs from the album had been hits for other artists and were recorded by him for the first time. "I'd Rather Be Sorry" and "I've Got to Have You," previously recorded by Sammi Smith and Carly Simon, are put on record by Kristofferson for the first time. The album exhibits a wide range of styles, with songs featuring popular, rock, soft rock, and country characteristics. "Lover Please" won a Grammy for the Best Country Vocal Performance by a Duo or a Group for 1975.

In 1975, Monument Records released Kristofferson's sixth solo album, *Who's to Bless and Who's to Blame*, whose songs, as indicated in the album title, largely have to do with moral dilemmas. All nine new songs were written by Kristofferson, who, notwithstanding his demanding schedule, had composed songs in a variety of musical styles. The diversity of subject and style within the songs contributed to the appeal and accessibility of the album. Also, it contained two novelty songs, one by the name of "Rocket to Stardom," about a security camera installed outside Kristofferson's Malibu home, before which countless desperately ambitious souls would perform in hopes he might be interested in them. The other, "Don't Cuss the Fiddle," is a tongue-and-cheek ditty serenading musicians who steal each other's songs. A confessional musician who sings what he feels, Kristofferson rambles through persistent preoccupations and moral and ethical musings, not to mention occasional love songs. In an unusual effort, this album contains a lengthy allegorical narrative, "Silver (The Hunger)," that elaborates the need for "deception and disguise." Interestingly enough, the song returns to his use of dramatic details, abstraction, and alliterative wordplay. Within the framework of the album, the song's examination of reality versus appearance contributes to the difficulties set forth in the album's title. Perhaps Kristofferson sees these moral uncertainties as songs that should naturally follow the confusion of success. The best-known song on this album is "Stranger," recorded very successfully by Johnny Duncan and Janie Fricke a few years later.

4

"THE GOING UP WAS WORTH THE COMING DOWN"

1977–1984

By 1975, Kristofferson had recorded five solo albums. He was actively pursuing writing and recording songs in addition to touring and promoting his albums. He was happily married to a wife who shared his interests, and they were parents of a child he adored. He also enjoyed a second career in film, which had developed from 1969, when Kristofferson met Dennis Hopper at the Troubadour Lounge in Los Angeles and was asked to participate in Hopper's film to be made in Peru. Although Kristofferson's intention to score the film did not materialize, he eventually "strums a mournful version of 'Bobby McGee' and speaks a single line" (Nelson, 1). Having directed the huge countercultural success, *Easy Rider* (1969), Hopper was allowed to make a personal project, the nonlinear allegorical *Last Movie* (1971), which was never widely distributed and eventually lost. After this experience, Kristofferson continued to act in films, many of which, such as his second film, *Cisco Pike*, included his songs on the sound track.

Having had no training, Kristofferson did well in certain parts and continued to be sought by directors. In 1973, he played Billy the Kid in Sam Peckinpah's *Pat Garrett and Billy the Kid* and convinced Bob Dylan, who wrote the music, most notably "Knocking on Heaven's Door," to join in. In 1974, Kristofferson worked with director Martin Scorsese in *Alice Doesn't Live Here Anymore*; Scorsese later gave him a boost in *Taxi Driver* (1976), with Robert DeNiro's and Cybill Shepherd's characters speaking of his album *The Silver Tongued Devil and I* (1971) in a record store. In 1975, he signed on with Sarah Miles and director Lewis John Carlino for *The Sailor Who Fell from Grace with the Sea*, a film based on the book by the same name written by Yukio Mishima. Set in Japan, the story was cinematically transferred to the coast of England—a circumstance that obscured much of Mishima's cultural preoccupation. Kristofferson's "Sea Dream Theme" shared the sound track with Johnny Mandel's music, forming a striking counterpart to Douglas Slocombe's superb cinematography. While the film's chilling ending tends to alienate viewers, critical response to it was positive, as was the reaction to Kristofferson's performance.

He enjoyed acting and learning about it, and it gave him an opportunity to express himself at another level and bring in more money at a time when his record sales were dropping. *Spooky Lady's Sideshow* was dismissed by most critics as a lapse in his creative powers, in that its lyrics move even farther from those of the earlier albums in both perspective and production. All of Kristofferson's recordings, beginning with his fourth album, were compared with his earlier songs and, of course, found wanting. Apparently, it was presumed he would continue to write classic songs of loneliness and alienation forever, just like those first songs in Nashville whose originality struck a lasting chord with the musical public. *Spooky Lady's Sideshow* has only more recently been seen to bear any real relation to the stress of his success and his frustration with the limitations placed on his time and creativity, all clearly striking fewer chords with his audience. Many of the nightmarish aspects of his touring were self-imposed by his staunch belief in his own personal freedom, from which he insisted fiercely that he had the right to do whatever he wanted. His alcoholism and substance abuse, which became for a while a badge of distinction, in that he was following Hank Williams and Johnny Cash in their attraction to the self-destructive flame, impressed upon him the assumption that any performer not living on the edge was not worth his salt. He sloshed his way through concerts and film roles, always needing alcohol to perform and always believing he was in control and could "handle it," no matter how close he was to the edge.

In 1976, in a fast-paced, minor film, *Vigilante Force*, he portrayed a Vietnam veteran who was hired to restore order in a small town taken over by oil-field workers. But the same year, he began his most significant role to date that launched him to a whole new level of fame. *A Star Is Born* had been acquired by Barbra Streisand, whom Kristofferson had met at the Troubadour, and her boyfriend, Jon Peters, as a vehicle for her powerful talents. For the third reincarnation of the famous story, Frank Pierson was slated to assume the helm, while for the male lead, Streisand sought an established rock star to portray a self-destructive rock-and-roll singer whose career was in decline. Rebuffed in her quest for Elvis Presley by his manager, Colonel Tom Parker, she had considered other performers but chose Kristofferson. Although he performed in "Watch Closely, Now," "Hellacious Acres," "Crippled Crow," "Lost Inside of You," and minimally in "Evergreen," he wrote no music for the film. Critic William Ruhlmann complained, "Kristofferson sounds even more gravelly than usual, and he isn't even growling his own compositions, which doubtless would have been superior to what he's been given to sing" (review of sound track to *A Star Is Born*). Paul Williams, who, with Streisand, wrote "Evergreen," spoke of his anxiety about writing and playing songs for Kristofferson: "I mean," he said, "this is the man who wrote 'Sunday Morning Coming Down,' 'Me and Bobby McGee.' . . . [but] Kris was great about the songs" (Williams). Stephen Miller adds that besides Williams and Streisand herself, the other writers included "Kenny Loggins, Leon Russell, Donna Weiss, and Kenny Ascher, who reflected her taste and left no room for Kristofferson's brand of intellectually crafted material. Even the harder-edged rock music was loaded with clichés" (148). Later, Kristofferson declared, "I liked *A Star Is Born* better than a lot of the critics. I wish I could have done the music for it but my publisher wouldn't split with Barbra and her producer so I had to do somebody else's songs" (Reid). For his performance in the film, Kristofferson won a Golden Globe for Best Actor in a Comedy or Musical, while Streisand was awarded a Golden Globe for Best Actress, and "Evergreen" won a Golden Globe, a Grammy, and an Oscar. The sound track for *A Star Is Born* sold 1.5 million copies worldwide.

During the making of the film, Kristofferson was, of course, drinking prodigious amounts of liquor while he was performing. He said, "I had a half-gallon of Jose Cuervo in my trailer and they never let it get empty. They just kept coming back in and filling it up, the same half-gallon. I don't know how much I was drinking, but it was a lot, and I had to quit soon after. [The] doctor said my liver was the size of a football" (Patterson, 3). Many assumed the drunkard he played in the film was himself. Liquor was largely responsible for his appearing nude in a pictorial layout with Sarah Miles in *Playboy*, presumably timed to parallel the release of *The Sailor Who Fell from Grace with the Sea*, in which he costarred with Miles. He later admitted that the incident occurred while he was drunk, and it was surely an embarrassment to Coolidge, who was unhappy with his continuous absence from home as well as his drunkenness and womanizing on the road. While watching *A Star Is Born*, Kristofferson was strongly affected by the film's ending. Seeing the death of his character and its devastating effect upon Streisand's character, he imagined the effect of his own death upon Coolidge and their young daughter. Cognizant of the state of his health from his years of boozing, he resolved to stop drinking.

The critical reception of *A Star Is Born* was not altogether favorable; many reviewers thought the film was too long (140 minutes), too boring, and too sappy. Comments concerning Kristofferson's performance varied, whereas the most savage criticism was set aside for Streisand, who was lambasted from various quarters. But despite the unkind pronouncements, the film was a box-office hit, ultimately grossing nearly $90 million worldwide, and "Evergreen" was one of the biggest hits of Streisand's career.

Doors began to open for Kristofferson that had been previously closed. He immediately became a sex symbol (at the age of forty) and came to be photographed frequently in shirts open to his navel. In the film industry, he came to be considered as a certain kind of character actor for staple roles that would carry him a long way. Possibly the most significant benefit from *A Star Is Born*'s completion was the time it freed for touring. Kristofferson and Coolidge promptly began a tour of more than thirty cities whose sold-out venues might well illustrate his move toward mainstream guaranteed by his role in the film. Also, they continued to make appearances on television variety shows, including Donny and Marie Osmond's showcase, *The Muppet Show*, and *Saturday Night Live*, keeping them extremely busy (Miller, 148–51). His *SNL* comedy began with Kristofferson on camera, sitting in a western set while holding a book he wrote, *Talk Country*. He says,

Howdy, I'm Kris Kristofferson. I guess you're wonderin' what a good old boy from Nashville is doin' on some tutti-frutti New York TV station. I mean, I make a pretty good livin'. I may not be no Bobby Dylan, but I don't go to work in the mornin'. You can do it too! Like a lot of you out there, I had a handicap. I was a college graduate with degrees in literature and creative writin', and I couldn't get arrested. Then how did I write songs that made me a legend in my time? The answer's in this book, *Talk Country*. It's got a chapter on nothin' but droppin' g's and another one on usin' double negatives, and one on grammar that tells why nobody wanted a song called "Sunday Mornin' Feelin' Terribly Depressed" or "Bobby McGee and I." Don't let your education stand in the way of stardom, or throw away a promisin' career because you can't say "ain't." Send five dollars and ninety-five cents to *Talk Country*. (Burke, 206)

To capitalize on his increased visibility in *A Star Is Born*, Monument released his solo seventh album, *Surreal Thing*, a collection of nine original songs with an album cover that backlights an outline of Kristofferson on a shadowy vehicle, suggesting an irrational blend of rider and performer. Completed a mere eight months after his sixth album, it includes "Killing Time" and "The Golden Idol," resurrected from Epic Records in 1967 and recut. Originally both sides of a single, the songs have a sixties Dylanesque disapproval frequently found in songs of that era. Following the same vein of criticism is "Eddie the Eunuch," a blast at a rock critic who compared him unfavorably with Jackson Browne, and the ire of "If You Don't Like Hank Williams," aimed squarely at critics who insist on categorizing him as either rock or country. The zealous "I've Got a Life of My Own" posits resolutely the choice of freedom made at the expense of everything else. The song concerns a speaker who refuses to be part of "a plan," insisting on living his own life. Hit viciously with a beer bottle, he retaliates, singing, "I had a knife of my own." In prison, he is left "alone and alive," and he still sings, "I've got a life of my own."

Kristofferson also included a few traditional love songs, one titled "It's Never Gonna Be the Same Again," which laments the end of a love affair. "I'm sorry we can't even still be friends," the speaker says, "but trusting you has left some wounds / That time ain't gonna mend." Wishing there was a way "that we could take it back to where it used to be," the speaker admits that "everything I used to make believe" now lies in pieces. Released as a single and intended for possible popularity, "It's Never Gonna Be the Same Again" never made the smallest impact upon public consciousness; it merely faded from view. Another love song, "Bad Love Story," sounding much like a country music song, concerns a man who keeps finding himself playing the same part in every love story; he has "had to learn [the story] by heart / 'cause I've lived these lines so many times before," and he finds it so sad the way the ending "still tears [him] apart / where the lady still don't love me anymore."

Produced by David Anderle, the album incorporates backing musicians on guitars, drums, bass, and keyboards, while including twelve backup singers on vocals. It seemed yet another experimental approach to the best way to present Kristofferson and his songs to the musical public. Bill Friskics-Warren says that Kristofferson's multifaceted career was difficult to categorize, as he had become a "strange mélange of Hollywood beefcake/millionaire, hipster Renaissance man, and poet laureate of country music" (9). Miller observes the production of his albums in the seventies suggests that "those in control were not quite sure what to do with this unusual and idiosyncratic talent, and continually filled tracks up with new sounds—vocal and instrumental—in an attempt to inject life into the project" (155). He adds that this uncertainty carried over into record stores where "retailers were unsure as to where to rack his albums" (155). The different presentations appeared to be endless variants of attempts to disguise his voice, yet avoiding the realization that he was more effective as a singer-songwriter in making a direct emotional connection with his audience.

In the spring of 1977, Monument sought again to take advantage of Kristofferson's prominence in his film career, having won a Golden Globe for his role in *A Star Is Born*, but whose career as a recording artist was perceived to be on the wane. As his most recent albums, *Who's to Bless and Who's to Blame* and *Surreal Thing*, had failed to meet expectations, the recording company released Kristofferson's first compilation, *Songs of Kristofferson*. The collection includes his four number 1 songs ("Me and Bobby McGee," "Help Me Make It through the Night," "Sunday Morning Coming Down," and "For the Good Times") from his debut album, *Kristofferson*, presented on one side, and on the other are "The Silver Tongued Devil and I"; "Loving Her Was Easier (Than Anything I'll Ever Do Again)," his first song to attain popular hit status; "The Pilgrim, Chapter 33" from his second album, *The Silver Tongued Devil and I*; and "Why Me" from the fourth album, *Jesus Was a Capricorn*. Two tracks from each of the final two albums completed the selections in the compilation, ensuring that the majority of them are his earlier and most successful works. Presumably the musical public appreciated having his most well-known songs together in one album, because it sold very well and eventually attained gold status.

After his first four albums, reviewers and critics had complained that album sales were decreasing and the quality of the songs was to blame. While many seemed to attribute this decline to the transfer of his primary energies to his film career leaving little time for the songwriting excellence of former days, others saw the real culprit as his recording contract with Monument Records that called for ten albums of original songs over a ten-year period, forcing him to write songs hurriedly.

While Kristofferson usually responded to criticism by insisting he wanted to go in different directions musically, he bemoaned to Tom Burke about his creative predicament: "I don't know anymore where . . . I am going. . . . Also, I'm unsure of my poems now. I have been since my *Spooky Lady Sideshow* album. Bob Hillburn, the critic who really made me when I started . . . wrote that those songs were my weakest. And I thought they were my best! I think I'm out of touch somehow. Creatively, I'm dog tired." When Burke suggested that Kristofferson remove himself from film and, "for a year, study, and write until the lyrics are right again," he replied, "I wish . . . that I was secure enough to believe that if I did that, and then wanted to come back, and found I couldn't, that it wouldn't tear me up" (Burke, 210).

Throughout the fall of 1977, Kristofferson was quite busy. He was inducted into the Nashville Songwriters Association International's Hall of Fame in recognition of his earlier work; he received a "Manny" (manuscript), a bronze cast of a hand holding a quill pen. Bob Beckham accepted Kristofferson's award on his behalf, as he was in New Orleans for the premiere of his latest film, Michael Ritchie's *Semi-Tough*, with Burt Reynolds and Jill Clayburgh. Kristofferson and Coolidge visited Nashville for the first time in four years, with much publicity and a display of goodwill toward their returning superstar. They were feted with receptions, cocktail parties, and a three-hour concert featuring Kristofferson and numerous guest artists.

Early in 1978, Kristofferson wrote, "I'm proud of this one," in the liner notes of *Easter Island*, his eighth solo album. It contained ten original songs, per his contract's specification, that had enjoyed more than eighteen months of coming to fruition, as opposed to half that amount of time for many of his other songs. Also, he had turned to Stephen Bruton and Mike Utley in a collaborative effort for four of the songs, and Mike Utley and Shel Silverstein in two others, with Kristofferson receiving sole credit for four songs on his "solo" album. In the title track he sings of the secrets locked in the ancient statues on Easter Island, seeing them "stranded like dogs in a star-spangled manger," and seeing in them "a dream that a world quit believing." Kristofferson ponders the incomplete nature of the statues, saying, "Surely the death of so grand an illusion / left us with legends too great to ignore" in that the images are still lost in what they came to explore. Confronted with such obscure imagery at the beginning of an album recorded in the eighth year of his successful career, one looks to the succeeding songs for any disillusionment or loss of vision that may have become a determining factor for this album. "Risky Bizness" involves the speaker and his opponent preparing for a title fight to determine the better one, while the speaker muses that "the best you can do is buy some time" before the inevitable dethroning. He continues, saying that with knowing "you have been the best that you could be," you can "make them fight to take the title you defend"; after you've "laid it on the line," the only option is to "Give 'em hell, boy," but still, "It's a risky bizness." With a hint of concern for his own status as an artist, Kristofferson, in "The Fighter," appears to consider his friend and songwriter, Billy Joe Shaver, whose storied life and career is the basis of his depiction in the song. Associated with the image of the "old fighter, tired and in trouble," Shaver carries on: once, after missing a performance, he showed up later sick from a spider bite "and crazy to look in the eye"; his performance was very sad, "and nobody even knew why." Kristofferson portrays Shaver as a clown "laughing like crazy," with "empty and deep" eyes.

The love songs bring a somewhat more firm foundation to the album, if only to identify an area not quite succumbing to the disillusionment or cynicism that continues to emerge through other albums to this one. "How Do You Feel About Fooling Around," later released in 1984 on the sound track to *Songwriter*, a film starring Kristofferson and

Willie Nelson, attempts playfully to interest someone in a bit of tenderness; Kristofferson says, "You'll never know 'til you try," implying it may very well lead to something lasting. "Lay Me Down (and Love the World Away)" stresses love as the antidote to the pressures and disappointments of pursuing fame and fortune: "I'm so glad that you're so glad to see my face again / That's all that's important anyway." "Forever in Your Love" repledges faith and trust from one to another after recognizing much change since their beginning: "And now you're free to be to / Be the best that you can be now." The speaker says that even if their dreams remain unfulfilled, "I still believe in you." "The Bigger the Fool, the Harder They Fall" sends a message to someone who has changed dramatically. The speaker admits he has continued to see her through the "old illusions and some make believe," while "closing my eyes to changes I've refused to see." "If someday you wake up in a world that's turned on you," where no one listens or answers, he says. "Hey, think of the easy dreamer who believes in you / The bigger the fool, the harder they fall." Also appearing as a strange love story is "Sabre and the Rose," a ballad-like account of riding with Stagger Lee, who determines that everyone is going into town "because the fairest ones in sight are blooming every night at a tavern / called the Sabre and the Rose." That night, the speaker says, "the light was crimson and I found her . . . all we had in common was our chains." Hearing orders ring out to "burn it to the ground, boys," he says, "All the way she ran holding to my hand / Running for the river and our life"; they swam to a spot they could never be found, he continues, and "all we left behind us was our clothes / and the stories, children." "Spooky Lady's Revenge" speaks of a former sideshow person who has risen to the top, leaving all her fears behind as she arrives "on the wings of her song." She is a shining star, "but she's hard in the heart like a diamond / flashing fire—cold as ice." "Living Legend," included in *The Highwaymen II* (1990), adds to the unconventional nature of the album through its suggestion of outlaws.

But critics continued in their disparagement. Paul Nelson of *Rolling Stone* carped contemptuously that *Easter Island* is not really a disaster, but "it's a barely mediocre record, one short step up from the bottom" (71). *Allmusic*'s William Ruhlmann said the "portents seemed good for Kris Kristofferson's eighth album": because of his increased visibility thanks to *A Star Is Born*; a good reception for his compilation album, *Songs of Kristofferson*; and the generous amount of eighteen months he had for writing the songs, Kristofferson had ensured success for the album. However, Ruhlmann said Kristofferson combined "ponderous, highly poetic compositions with several commercial-sounding love songs," and the album only "marked a slight improvement over [his] recent sales" (Ruhlmann, review of *Easter Island*). Numerous reviewers persisted in their complaints of a troubling decline in the quality of Kristofferson's work involving the imagery and ideas, and his continuing preoccupation with the down side of touring, generally focusing on the sordid if not more lurid experiences. Critics lamented a lost output of standards regarding his seventies albums, and while many followers shrank from the repetition of themes, imagery, and wordplay, they also found little connection with the reiteration of life on the road. The reality of basic human need, once so abundant in his songs and easily felt by his listeners, had largely disappeared. However much the argument might be made that, despite the objectionable elements found in his songs of the late seventies, they too resonate with loneliness, disillusionment, and cynicism as well as other common human emotions, nevertheless, with every album's release, fewer copies were sold.

Perhaps the disappointment took its toll on Kristofferson, or as William Ruhlmann suggests, "he must have considered his recording career as an afterthought to his more prominent career in the movies," because his ninth original songs solo album, *Shake Hands with the Devil*, contained mostly previously written songs (review of *Shake Hands with the Devil*). Many of them written years before 1979, they were quite possibly chosen for their application in theme and mood to his shaky marriage. "Whiskey, Whiskey," a cover of Tom Ghent's 1970 hit for Nat Stuckey, bewails the fact that his love is a "little bit like the weather"; he never knows "when she's gonna change." Because "she's a part of my heart / and a whole lot of my pain," he turns to "whiskey, whiskey my old friend," and asks of it to "please be kind / Drive this feeling from my mind." He goes on to say, "Somehow her smile" can "let the sun shine in," but now he realizes he's been blinded "by the cold and wintery wind" that was masterfully "disguised behind her eyes." He cries out, "Oh, what a fool I've been," just before going into the refrain, "Whiskey, whiskey my old friend / I've come to talk with you again." "Come Sundown," Kristofferson's song from 1970, had been a hit for Bobby Bare (who had a more agreeable voice than Kristofferson's) and seems here to anticipate the misery of Kristofferson's ap-

proaching separation: in the song, the speaker is awakened by the closing of the front door, signifying the departure of his love from his life.
He realizes it's over and knows the hurt is yet to come: "Cause this
morning, she's just leavin', but come sundown, she'll be gone." "Once
More with Feeling," also written in 1970 and a hit for Jerry Lee Lewis,
describes the speaker's realization that his partner is merely "going
through the motions . . . never quite together like before." Aware that
"something good / got lost along the way," and looking for ways to
restore their union, the speaker says, "Let's try it one more time"; as he
guides her toward believability, he observes that while she is touching
him as she once did, she is "looking everywhere but in [his] eyes." He
finally encourages her to go for the most important aspect of it all:
"Darling, make believe you're making me / believe each word you say."
The only new song Kristofferson wrote on the album is "Prove It to You
One More Time Again," a heartbreaking attempt to salvage a relationship; he says, "I can't believe that you still don't believe in me," and
pleads to keep going, insisting, "We gotta try / and do the story true
right to the end." In the title track, the speaker denies being the devil or
a saint, but he wants to get someone away from the world and will do
whatever that takes. He says bluntly that if that makes him a devil,
shake his hand, but adds that "I'm not after anything you don't want to
give me."

At the time when Kristofferson's recording career was declining—
although his film career was prospering—Rita Coolidge's solo recording
career was moving upward. She had recorded in 1977 *Anytime . . .
Anywhere*, which had reached platinum status, and *Love Me Again*,
reaching gold, all a far cry from her first duo with Kristofferson, which
increased her visibility and marketability through her association with
him. At the beginning of 1979, he and Coolidge released their third and
final duo, *Natural Act*, which contains songs by Kristofferson, Donnie
Fritts, Billy Swan, T-Bone Burnett, and Sonny Curtis. The stiff photos
of the pair on Annie Leibovitz's album cover have fostered speculative
comments regarding the state of their relationship. No more relaxed,
informal photos suggesting a closeness between them, photos on this
album front and back scream distance. "Loving Her Was Easier (Than
Anything I'll Ever Do Again)," usually dedicated to Coolidge, now is
sung as a duet; "Please Don't Tell Me How the Story Ends," a hit for
Ray Price back in 1970, displays beautiful harmonies on a sad song that

now seems prophetic; and the previously unrecorded "Love Don't Live Here Anymore" perhaps says more than was thought at the time: "Nothing's left between us but the space between us." Pieces of their marriage and lives lie scattered on the floor, no one has anything to say to anyone, and no connections are left other than the shredded emotional ones. Besides these three songs written by Kristofferson, the remainder of songs in the album were written by members of his band, his music producer, T-Bone Burnett, and others.

On March 2–4, 1979, Kristofferson and Coolidge participated in a three-day music festival held at the Karl Marx Theater in Havana, Cuba. Set in motion two years previously by U.S. president Jimmy Carter and Cuban president Fidel Castro as a cultural exchange by two enemy nations perhaps leading to further normalization of diplomatic relations between the two, the festival was finally in place with Weather Report, Stephen Stills, Bonnie Bramlett, Kris Kristofferson, Rita Coolidge, and Billy Joel for the American participating artists, Afro-Cuban jazz band Irakere, and other well-known groups. Dubbed Havana Jam, the festival was known only by word of mouth, and those attending, by invitation only, were cultural personalities, Communist officials, and some selected students. The performance, televised for both countries and recorded by CBS as a live double album, was seen as a representation of "music over politics," the idea behind its evolution. Bruce Lundvall, director of CBS Records, who worked on the concert's development, was overwhelmed by Cuban jazz on his trip to Cuba and was determined to work out a music collaborative effort between Cuba and the United States. As Kristofferson was known for his interest in Latin America, and Coolidge's songs were well known via AM radio, they were specifically chosen to facilitate good relations. Throughout his music career, Stephen Stills had experimented with Latin American music. Kristofferson sang "Living Legend," "You Show Me Yours and I'll Show You Mine," and "Blue as I Do," and Coolidge sang "The Way You Do the Things You Do" and "Your Love Has Lifted Me Higher," with most Cuban audience members singing along with her.

Kristofferson had accepted more parts in films—the part of Rubber Duck in the Sam Peckinpah–directed trucker movie *Convoy*, and *Freedom Road*, a film based on a novel by Howard Fast. In 1979, also, Kristofferson began work on *Heaven's Gate* (1980), Michael Cimino's gorgeously photographed yet lengthy and overly expensive film, whose overruns ultimately led to the demise of the studio. During the time Kristofferson was filming in Montana, Coolidge took Casey and left. Stunned and grieved by Coolidge's actions, he pictured his daughter, Casey, being removed from him much as were his children with Fran, his first wife, when they were taken to California and he, still in Nashville, saw them not at all for some time. In *Kris Kristofferson: His Life and Work*, director Cimino speaks of Kristofferson's black moods, with the divorce weighing on him, and how they actually worked to render a unique portrayal of his character in *Heaven's Gate*.

Ironically, when all of Kristofferson's albums following *A Star Is Born* were successively reviled by critics and were incapable of generating healthy sales, Willie Nelson released *Willie Sings Kristofferson* (1979), which reached gold status in Canada and platinum in the United States. Through the winter of 1979–1980, Kristofferson accompanied Nelson on a sellout tour that publicized the album and kept himself in public view.

With no tours or concerts of his own to consume his time, he took part in the television opportunities that came his way. In 1980, Kristofferson participated in a tribute to Johnny Cash. For the celebration titled *Johnny Cash: The First 25 Years*, guests included Dolly Parton, Waylon Jennings, Jack Clement, Carl Perkins, Kirk Douglas, Don Williams, and Anne Murray. Following the show, Johnny and June entertained two hundred guests at a gala event.

Later in the year, a two-hour television special, *Hank Williams: A Man and His Music*, aired. Hosted by Hank Williams Jr., it featured members of the original Drifting Cowboys, Williams's backing group; Kristofferson sang "I'm So Lonesome I Could Cry," Williams's standard that played such a part in Kristofferson's entry into country music. Written in 1949, the famous song about loneliness is at the top of the list; it is one of those of Williams's that Kristofferson fell in love with when he was thirteen.

In 1980, his tenth Monument solo album of original songs was released. Sixteen months after *Shake Hands with the Devil*'s uneventful introduction to the musical public, Kristofferson's final contracted album to Fred Foster and Monument Records was released. Produced by Norbert Putnam and featuring Donnie Fritts on keyboard and coauthor Billy Swan on guitar, *To the Bone* contains nine angry, anguished songs concerning his breakup with Coolidge. These are painful to listen to and were, no doubt, painful to perform as well. One song, "Daddy's Song," addresses the concerns of their five-year-old child; she says, "Daddy, it's breaking my heart." In the song, Kristofferson also has heartache; and as he returns to his lifelong theme, freedom, he acknowledges there is a freedom to being on one's own that's "nearly worth what you've paid." Another song, "Maybe You've Heard," addresses the rumormongers, asking for restraint in their condemnation of both parties involved. "You ought to know him, give him a hand, if you can," Kristofferson says. "He was your friend." To those critical of Coolidge, he says, "Don't you condemn her; leave it to strangers." And he repeats, "She was your friend."

Several of the songs address the partner, seeking clarification or renewed efforts to try again; some merely lament the desperate situation. In "Nobody Loves Anybody Anymore," the only song to inspire any real sales, Kristofferson says bitterly, "If it don't come easy, now / it ain't worth fighting for." "Last Time" states that "all there is left of our love is a little girl's laughter," and predicts "I'll never believe in forever again." To "Magdalene," he speaks about his pain and loneliness.

After this album dropped off the charts and out of sight, Kristofferson did not record a solo album for six years. Moreover, with the exception of *Rollover* (1981), with Jane Fonda and already in preproduction, the *Heaven's Gate* debacle ensured that he would not be considered for a leading-man part in any film for the next three years. The eclipse of his recording and acting careers was paralleled throughout by his personal desolation: in addition to the unwanted divorce, his longtime manager and also his agent had both passed away, and a tragedy was miraculously avoided much nearer home.

On tour in Europe, Kristofferson received word in April 1982 that his daughter Tracy, child of his first marriage to Fran, had been involved in a motorcycle accident in Lancaster, California, and was in critical condition. Riding behind Eric Heiden, winner of five gold medals in speed skating at the 1980 Winter Olympics, Tracy, a twenty-year-old student at Stanford University, was hit by a mobile home that crashed into the bike. At the hospital, Kristofferson and Fran waited through the hours while the doctors were learning of the extent of her injuries. Later, Kristofferson spoke of this experience:

I had just started sobering up and a friend of mine in AA told me that if you don't believe in God, ask for something impossible and stand back. He did this when my oldest daughter was in a motorcycle accident; she was unconscious and it looked as if she were paralyzed. I was in Europe on a concert tour at the time and all the way back I was making deals with God: please, no paralysis, no brain damage. I walked into the room and she was tied down to the table; she couldn't even recognize me. I wasn't there 15 seconds and the doctor said, "Look!" Her leg had moved. (Jordan)

Kristofferson's old friend and producer Fred Foster had incurred huge financial losses in a banking venture; consequently, both Monument and Combine recording studios faced bankruptcy. In 1982, in an effort to stem the tide of financial ruin and to show their appreciation to Foster, several former Monument artists joined together for a double-album compilation. Dolly Parton, Brenda Lee, Willie Nelson, and Kristofferson recorded *The Winning Hand*, an assortment of solos and duets involving new songs as well as old. Kristofferson sang seven duets and two solo songs. Among his duets are "Help Me Make It through the Night" with Brenda Lee, "Casey's Last Ride" with Willie Nelson, and "Ping Pong" with Dolly Parton. His solos are "The Bandits of Beverly Hills," and "Here Comes That Rainbow Again," written with John Steinbeck's *Grapes of Wrath* in mind as a reminder to listeners of his concern for the oppressed. Johnny Cash wrote copious liner notes recalling Kristofferson's arrival in Nashville back in 1965 and recounted his version of Kristofferson's notorious stunt landing a helicopter in Cash's yard in Nashville. All four artists appeared on a two-hour television special, hosted by Cash in 1983. *The Winning Hand* was quite successful, as it moved into the Country Top Five category.

Also in 1983, Kristofferson returned to Nashville for a weeklong celebration of his music, with Johnny Cash leading a special tribute at the Country Music Awards Show and singing a medley of Kristofferson classics with Anne Murray, Lee Greenwood, and Larry Gatlin. Later, Kristofferson gathered with old friends David Allan Coe, Roger Miller, Willie Nelson, and Mickey Newbury for a guitar pull; "It's been a long time since I stayed up all night playing music," he said, as quoted by Miller, "especially straight, so you remember what you did" (178).

Also in 1983, Kristofferson had been honored by a BMI, Broadcast Music Inc., banquet for five of his best-known songs that had accumulated over seven million airplays. Dressed in a tuxedo, he received standing ovations throughout the evening. He was looking much fitter than earlier and had become quite earnest about caring for Casey after the divorce, adopting the title of bachelor father. He had married again, this time to Lisa Meyers, an attorney he met in a Malibu gym. The ceremony took place on February 19, 1983, in the chapel at Pepperdine University, where Meyers had graduated.

In 1984, Kristofferson was finally able to move back into low-budget films and films for television. He accepted a part in a CBS movie, *The Lost Honor of Kathryn Beck*, a remake of the 1975 German film *The Lost Honor of Katharina Blum*, costarring Marlo Thomas as a woman who spends a night with a man with a shady past and as a result is harassed by the police and the press. The same year, Kristofferson participated in *Flashpoint*, directed by William Tannen, and also starring Rip Torn, Treat Williams, Tess Harper, and Roberts Blossom. The film concerns two border-patrol officers who discover an abandoned jeep full of money and a body from about the sixties; soon they are set upon by people who wanted the jeep to remain hidden, and a conspiracy seems to be ready for disclosure. Or is it? The film's music is provided by the German electronic band Tangerine Dream, to accompany the film's eerie, dark feel.

In 1984, Kristofferson joined Willie Nelson in the film *Songwriter*, written by Bud Shrake and directed by Alan Rudolph, protégé of Robert Altman. The offbeat film concerns Doc Jenkins (Nelson), a country music writer who enlists the help of his friend Blackie Buck (Kristofferson) in liberating him from his onerous entanglements with a disreputable producer; based loosely on Nelson's experiences, the narrative exposes considerable exploitation in the music industry as it follows the antics of two good old boys trying to survive in the business. Several movie critics were attracted to the film and praised its acting, direction, and music; Pauline Kael admired the character delineations throughout, while Roger Ebert was impressed by the film's unpredictability, rating it three and a half out of four stars.

To the *Songwriter* sound track, which received an Academy Award nomination but lost out to Prince's *Purple Rain*, Nelson and Kristofferson contributed eleven songs. Each side of the record is devoted to solos of one singer as well as a duet by both. The most popular song, "How Do You Feel About Fooling Around," written by Kristofferson,

Bruton, and Utley, and included in *Easter Island* in 1978, is a duet by the two that propelled it to the top of the country chart. Nelson's songs, the caustic "Write Your Own Songs" and "Who'll Buy My Memories," written to "Mr. Music Executive" and "Mr. Purified Country," and sung by Doc Jenkins, spotlight some of the difficulties singer-songwriters encounter in their negotiations with greedy businessmen seeking to fleece naive songwriters. Kristofferson's "Down to Her Socks" is a good country song about a "good ole girl with a big ole heart that got broke" because she loved "some son of a bitch who didn't love her back enough"; she finally saw the light, and although "it sure took a long time to go," she finally left. He declares that one day, "you wake up and look down at your feet and find they're just / walking you away." In "Eye of the Storm," Kristofferson recognizes someone who has been hurt and reminds him there are things to be grateful for. He says, "Thank God you still got your feelings," and insists that the person is still in the "peak of your form," or "the eye of the storm." "From here to the end is what matters, my friend"; he continues that the only difference between living and dying "is loving or leaving alone."

The other two songs Kristofferson wrote and sang for *Songwriter* are "Crossing the Border" and "Under the Gun," coauthored by Guy Clark, which have little if anything to do with the film but, as William Ruhlmann says, "a lot to do with the singer-songwriter's own current concerns" (review of *Music from Songwriter*). Already exercised by the U.S. government's interest in Central America, Kristofferson, remembering the lies about Vietnam, wrote disillusionment-driven music that exposed his incipient activism that would soon come into full bloom.

Although Kristofferson swore off drinking after he finished work on *A Star Is Born*, he did not achieve sobriety in 1976. He struggled with it for years, eventually entering practically every rehab in California for treatment. But the effects of his sobriety were obvious and beneficial. His appearance improved with some weight loss, and communication improved with his band, and in general with everyone. However, in Steve Earle's "Kris Kristofferson Story," Rita Coolidge asserted that his sobriety added to the trouble in their marriage as he had become a different person when sober, who was required to "deal with his life and issues as a sober person."

5

REBELS, OUTLAWS, HIGHWAYMEN
1985–1995

In late 1984, Kris Kristofferson, Johnny Cash, Willie Nelson, and Waylon Jennings got together in Montreux, Switzerland, to tape Cash's annual Christmas television special; afterward, they engaged in a friendly guitar pull and began to kick around the idea of the formation of a country music supergroup. While at Montreux, they all listened to Jimmy Webb's song "Highwayman," liked it, and later, in Nashville, laid down some tracks for it, with the idea of an album taking shape. The four foresaw touring together, instead of separately, with the added incentive of hanging out together.

Stephen Miller pondered the possible disastrous collision of four "uncompromising egos" but saw that the "fact that all, apart from Nelson, were in the commercial doldrums should provide powerful enough incentive to unite" (184). The four sought mostly to boost their careers that had been stymied by the state of country music at that time. Being edged out of the country music commercial scene by the younger so-called neotraditionalists that included artists like George Strait, Randy Travis, and Dwight Yoakum, followed by Clint Black, Garth Brooks, and Vince Gill, the middle-aged quartet of singers, unable to compete, proposed a supergroup of "outlaws" to jolt their sagging popularity. No real advocates of hard country, the neotraditionalists experimented with country, country-pop, and rock and roll and, as a result, enjoyed phenomenal revenues.

When singer-songwriter Lee Clayton penned "Ladies Love Outlaws" and sang it, his friend Kris Kristofferson, who was impressed, said, "Sounds to me like you've just written ole Waylon a hit song." Clayton replied, "Why shouldn't it be a hit for ole Waylon? It was, after all, written about him, and besides, the song has one hell of a hook." Indeed. And as Michael Bane continues the story, "Waylon was impressed, too. He named a whole album after it in 1972. The hook had worked, and the term 'outlaw' was now in circulation" (*Outlaws*, 4). Instead of "progressive music," outlaw music seemed to fit the musicians who in the 1960s and 1970s fought the studios, perceived as the enemy, for the right to make music the way they wanted. Clayton's term "outlaw" is still associated with the movement that sought to avoid the limitations of the Nashville sound, with its simple songs overwhelmed with studio musicians and lush instrumentation, that allowed no room for the artists' production preferences. The movement had begun the year before when Willie Nelson, at a low period in his life, left Nashville for his home state of Texas to begin again his career in Austin at the Armadillo World Headquarters. It was there that the hippies and rednecks formed a significant blend in Nelson's youthful audience; it was also there that Nelson changed his image to fit his audience. Both Jennings and Nelson battled the Nashville country music establishment famously, with each becoming a leader in outlaw music.

Outlaws exist in the fantasies of a great many people. In his book, *Outlaw: Waylon, Willie, Kris, and the Renegades of Nashville*, Michael Streissguth speaks of the outlaw ethos in America, noting that "romantic bandits such as Jesse James, Billy the Kid, and Pretty Boy Floyd galloped through the national imagination with a zeal that had faded little since that dirty Robert Ford plugged James in the back of the head at St. Joseph, Missouri, in 1882" (152). Streissguth notes the role played by the "yellow journalists and pulp historians" in assigning purer motives for criminal actions and transforming evildoers into Robin Hoods who help "families in need." America's identification with the outlaw mythos was reflected in the 1960s and 1970s in its celebration in popular culture through films such as *Bonnie and Clyde*, *Easy Rider*, and *Butch Cassidy and the Sundance Kid*, along with the great popularity of Johnny Cash's *At Folsom Prison* and Bob Dylan's *John Wesley Harding* (Streissguth, 152).

The whole idea of outlaw music essentially unfolded through the styles of various artists whose defiance of certain conventions fanned the flames of outlawry. Over the years, certain aspects of the musicians considered outlaws had individually evolved into keen representations of how they wanted to be perceived, with the appearance of each artist embodying the freedom he demanded in his music—all of which contributed immensely to his popular appeal as an outlaw. The singer-songwriters in Nashville in the 1970s longed to escape the traditional role of the recording artist and enjoy the freedom of Bob Dylan, the Beatles, Rolling Stones, and other rock artists who wrote their own material and participated in creative decisions about their albums. But the country music industry, under threat from rock and roll, created the Country Music Association (CMA) to increase the number of country music radio stations and adopted the smoother Nashville sound that was suggested as a profitable endeavor by market researchers, thereby forcing the artists to remain tethered to its formulaic design for making money. Consequently, while the term "outlaw" suggests existing outside the law and engaging in rebellious behavior, the true meaning of the term in the music context lies in a recording artist's rebellion against the recording company's attempted control of his or her music.

On *We Walk the Line: The Tribute to the Music of Johnny Cash*, on August 2, 2012, Willie Nelson said, "I always looked at John as somebody who had been there before me and had done it the way he wanted to do it. I always admired and respected him for doing that. He was one of the first rebels, one of the first outlaws . . . that hit Nashville" (Dunkerley). When Cash left Sun Records in Memphis, arriving in Nashville in the late 1950s, he had more latitude than most in following his own inclinations. His recording "I Walk the Line" had already reached a million in sales, and his relationship with Columbia Recording Studio was such that during Kristofferson's employment there in 1966, he recorded whenever he chose, frequently slipping into the studio in the wee hours to record at night. He had skirmishes with producers who ignored his preference for stripped-down sound, insisting his recordings include more guitars and violins to achieve the Nashville sound. He chose his own topics, traditional or no, and brooked no interference with the Tennessee Three, his backing band of the renowned boom-chicka-boom rhythm. Generally speaking, he called the shots, with the exception of allowing the producer to choose the songs for his LP *John*

R. Cash (1974), a concession he saw as a mistake. He later said, "I went through the mid-70s doing my own thing, staying away from politics on Music Row, making my own albums my way." He would not let that mistake occur again (Hamilton). Cash also dressed as he pleased, becoming the man in black, and assumed that label as one who acknowledged the world's injustices, and according to Patrick Carr, he chose that stage attire as a "symbol of rebellion against a stagnant status quo . . . against hypocritical houses of God, [and] against people whose minds are closed to others' ideas" (Cash, with Carr, 64).

Cash first achieved outlaw status from his notoriety for heavy drinking and addiction to amphetamines, which he had begun to stay awake while touring on the road, and barbiturates. When he first came to Nashville, he shared an apartment briefly with Waylon Jennings, whose exploits were legendary. Cash's performances in Folsom Prison and San Quentin Prison gave rise to the rumor, apparently believed by a large number of people, that he had been incarcerated in prison. His arrests for setting fire to a U.S. national forest, picking flowers in a restricted area, and for prescription drug offenses on two occasions—all misdemeanors, for which he served a total of seven nights in jail—continued to fuel rumors of his incarceration. Jonathan Silverman, in *Nine Choices: Johnny Cash and American Culture*, suggests that Cash allowed the manipulation of information about his rumored incarceration to encourage its truth in fact, thereby increasing his outlaw status and adding to his fame.

Cash irked the Music Row establishment with the practice on his television show (1969–1971) of welcoming not just country music artists but also various counterculture artists, specifically rock musicians, including Bob Dylan, Joni Mitchell, Eric Clapton, Neil Young, and others, and promoting them to the world. In the words of Michael Streissguth, "Johnny Cash forced change on country music" (67). In April 1971, Cash planned to debut a version of Kristofferson's song "Sunday Morning Coming Down," with an impressive arrangement, on his show, that would provide a huge career assist for Kristofferson as well as a personal endorsement from an artist he had long idolized. Stephen Deusner, of *American Songwriter*, writes of this event: "However, ABC executives objected to one line in the song: 'Wishin,' Lord, that I was stoned.' Instead, they suggested an alternative that would be potentially less offensive to straight-laced viewers who might recoil at even the hint of turning on: 'Wishin,' Lord, that I was home.'" Both Cash and Kristofferson thought about it, talked about it, and realized that the "line was crucial to the song's evocation of alienation and loneliness, a feeling so strong that even 'home' might not alleviate the misery." But what Cash would do was not known. However, at the taping, "Cash took the stage at the Ryman and intoned, in that familiar basso profundo, that he wished, "Lord, that he was stoned" (Deusner, 1).

Deusner goes on to say,

> That is a crucial performance in country music history. On one hand, it represents one generation of country singers passing the torch to the next, an act that cemented Kristofferson's reputation as the genre's top songwriter. Moreover, it validated the surging outlaw movement, a group of musicians who bristled against the practices of the industry and the formal constraints of the genre. . . . Kristofferson wrote meandering melodies and songs that far exceeded the typical two or three minutes. Even the subject matter changed, as outlaw hits explored frank depictions of sexual need (Kristofferson's "Help Me Make It through the Night") and cheeky commentary on the scene itself (Waylon Jennings's "Don't You Think This Outlaw Bit's Done Got Out of Hand?"). (2)

Despite Waylon Jennings's victory over RCA Nashville, he was really not the first outlaw; that distinction belongs to Johnny Cash, and Kris Kristofferson, who was also a leader in the outlaw movement before it actually began. The deterioration of Kristofferson's appearance, from the clean-cut army captain to a disheveled songwriter performing janitorial duties at Columbia Recording Studio, washing dishes, tending bar, hanging out in the streets and bars, and pitching his songs to anyone who would listen, was a sharp signal of his diminished status. Having no contract with any studio before Fred Foster at Monument Records, Kristofferson attracted attention with his songwriting, creating songs of uncommon lyrical depth and beauty. He was, however, prevented from recording them because of his craggy voice, and they were instead recorded by A-list singers with melodious voices. When Johnny Cash's recording of "Sunday Morning Coming Down" led to Kristofferson's CMA award for the 1970 Song of the Year, his behavior before the august assemblage caused a stir. With his unkempt and scruffy appearance, he was seen by many Music Row executives as a disgrace and by some as unfit for the award. However, the establishment felt perhaps even more scandalized by his song lyrics that probed honest emotions and relationships, and refused to rely on clichés, vague phrases, or rhymes used traditionally in country music to represent more intense feelings. Perceived as a hippie lacking the proper respect and bent on undermining long-standing values, he outraged a number of leading artists. But as Kristofferson chose country music because he felt he could find self-expression there, he insisted upon speaking honestly and on having the freedom to speak honestly. By opposing those in the music business in Nashville who would deny him the right to freedom of expression, he forged the name of outlaw for himself that paved the way for others who would fight for their rights.

With respect to the four Highwaymen as representations of outlaws, Kristofferson said,

> I don't think that would've been the broad name we would've chosen. To be outlaws. I think we went our own way and spoke our own words because we believed in them. And believed that's what we were set down on the planet to do. We weren't worried about commerciality. Because it didn't make any difference if we were on the Hit Parade or whether we were making a lot of money. It was whether we were doing good work . . . writing soulful songs. (*They Called Us Outlaws* [documentary])

When Willie Nelson recorded his first album in Nashville, after playing in dance halls and honky-tonks for ten years in Texas, and after having written several of his more noteworthy songs and sold some of them for mere pittances, he was hired as a staff writer at Pamper Music, a song publishing company, and was paid $50 a week. After a short time, he had written "Crazy," "Hello Walls," and "Funny How Time Slips Away," sung variously by Patsy Cline, Faron Young, Elvis Presley, and Ray Charles. In 1964, he signed on with Fred Foster at Monument and, following the taping of five songs, left Monument abruptly for RCA. After seven mediocre years at RCA, he returned to Austin and performed for a huge diverse audience at the Armadillo World Headquarters, whereupon, in the words of Bill Malone, he "began making a calculated attempt to appeal to young people, and particularly to those who had grown up with rock music and had been touched by counterculture values" (Malone and Neal, 396). Forsaking RCA's lack of interest in promoting his music and the dearth of performing venues in Nashville, Nelson exchanged his performance attire of a turtleneck sweater and a blazer for jeans and tennis shoes. To complete his outlaw regalia, he added a headband and an earring, along with red, white, and blue scarves and hats that proclaimed his patriotism while, like most of his musical audience, eschewed an alliance with any political party. In 1973, he was pursued by Atlantic Records on the strength of his song-writing and his great popularity in Texas. After finding his relationship with Atlantic unsatisfactory, he went to Columbia, home of artists un-suitable for Nashville mainstream, and, in 1975, recorded in an Austin studio tapes for *Red Headed Stranger*. When Columbia executives real-ized that no other instrumentation would be added to the very sparse amount there, and Nelson's contract required its release as it was, they agreed grudgingly, expecting a flop. To their surprise, the album, link-ing up with America's fondness for the western outlaw, became a huge hit and was certified gold in 1976; also, Nelson's cover of Fred Rose's song from the 1940s, "Blue Eyes Crying in the Rain," became a number 1 single. Nelson's concept album relates the story of a man who be-comes a fugitive after he kills his wife and her lover; the reviews were mostly enthusiastic, and Nelson was recognized by *New York Times* music critic John Rockwell as an outlaw with a national audience. *News-week* pronounced him the king of country music, and he adorned the cover of *Rolling Stone*.

Outlaw music came into prominence in 1976 with *Wanted: The Out-laws*, featuring Waylon Jennings, Jessi Colter, Tompall Glaser, and Wil-lie Nelson as outlaws. "The cover was Pure Old West," says Jennings, "a yellowed reward poster with the stagecoach air of the nineteenth-centu-ry frontier, Dodge City to Tombstone" (Jennings and Kaye, 220). While trying to engineer a hit for Jennings that would provide some competi-tion for Willie Nelson's phenomenally successful album, *Red Headed Stranger* (1975), Jerry Bradley, head of RCA in Nashville, visualized the album and its title, unaware of a Southern rock band already operating under the same name. Containing previously published material by all four artists, *Wanted: The Outlaws* made history as the first country album to sell a million copies. The LP was named the Country Music Association's Album of the Year for 1976, and Nelson and Jennings were awarded Duo of the Year by the CMA for their hit single from the LP, "Good Hearted Woman."

Following RCA's release of *Wanted: The Outlaws, Waylon and Willie* (1978), another best-selling album that included "Mammas Don't Let Your Babies Grow Up to Be Cowboys," continued a focus on Waylon and Willie as outlaws. Nelson's autonomy allowed him to record a diversity of musical styles, including gospel and older songs, thereby welcoming a number of older listeners outside country. In 1977, he recorded *To Lefty, From Willie*, a tribute to country artist Lefty Frizzell that celebrated honky-tonk roots; and in 1978, he surprised his audience with a sharp turn into pop standards with *Stardust*, an LP that sold millions.

Waylon Jennings, who began his career playing bass with fellow Texan Buddy Holly, came to Nashville and RCA from Phoenix, after performing rockabilly for four years. His appearance still resembled 1950s singers who wore tight jeans and high-collared shirts, but Chet Atkins pushed him immediately into folk and pop-country music where he won a Grammy for his recording of "MacArthur Park," with the Kimberleys. Atkins returned to playing guitar, leaving Jennings in the hands of his new producer, Danny Davis, who proceeded to overdub everything Jennings recorded. His requests for change or for a different drumbeat would always be refused. He found a powerfully effective lawyer who squeezed a fat, new contract from RCA, giving him his own production company. "This meant," says Neil Hamilton, "he had control of his music: the advertising, the promotion, and the mixing. He even began recording with his band, The Waylors, in the studio he wanted, one owned by . . . Tompall Glaser, rather than RCA's. Jennings had made his choice, and with it he began propelling a revolution in country music" (90–91).

When Jennings recorded *Ladies Love Outlaws* in 1972, the album cover sported a photograph of him in black with a six-gun—the object of the admiration of a young girl. "From this point on," says Bill Malone, "'outlaw' began to replace 'rebel' as a descriptive term for Jennings and his music" (400). In 1973, Jennings recorded *Honky Tonk Heroes*, all songs but one written by Billy Joe Shaver and having a ragged edge; "There Ain't No God in Mexico" used only three instruments, achieving a simplicity that "was the ultimate kick . . . to the Nashville sound," says Hamilton (91).

Hamilton states, "For the Outlaws, artistic freedom was their West and their piece of land" (90). "We were rebels," Jennings explained, "but we didn't want to dismantle the system. We just wanted our own patch" (Jennings and Kaye, 222). As he moved closer to that freedom, his appearance changed to include longer hair, a beard (already considerably underway because of a hospital stay), and scruffy clothes.

Jennings's edgy, gritty lyrics touted their honky-tonk roots, an important aspect of country music. He loved a heavy bass with an emphasis on the downbeat and a steady, accented beat in 4/4 time, a musical style he had favored in all the honky-tonks he had played in before he came to Nashville. However, his musical model, as with many country artists, was Hank Williams, his outlaw hero. Much like Kristofferson, Jennings too had been touched when he was a young boy by Williams, "through the strength of his songs and the soul of his voice. I especially loved his Luke the Drifter recitations, morality tales like 'Pictures from Life's Other Side' or 'Too Many Parties and Too Many Pals.' . . . Everything I did in Nashville, anything *anyone* did was measured against Hank's long, lanky shadow" (224). He said, "We wanted to be like him, romanticizing his faults, fantasizing ourselves lying in a hotel room sick and going out to sing" (226). Jennings's song "Are You Sure Hank Done It This Way," written and recorded in 1975, played upon the obsessive following of Williams. But Jennings said,

> With its relentless four-on-the-floor rhythm, phased guitars, and eerie drones, "Hank" didn't sound like a standard country record. There was no clear-cut verse and chorus, no fiddle middle break, no bridge, nothing but an endless back-and-forth seesaw between the two chords. Jack mixed the guitars together so they sounded like one huge instrument, matching their equalization settings so you couldn't tell where one blended into the other. (227)

"It felt like a different music, and Outlaw was as good a description as any," declared Jennings, who like most traditional country singers, resented Nashville's turn into pop music (the CMA had named Olivia Newton-John its Female Vocalist of the Year for 1974), and sensed a "mood that was craving our message of freedom and a fresh start." Outlaw music had come to represent country music underground, and the public, liking what it heard, gave a strong welcome to *Wanted: The Outlaws*.

With regard to playing the music inside him, Jennings said, "When I put the black hat on and walked to the stage carrying my Telecaster, I was staking out my own piece of land where the buffalo roam" (221). Not unexpectedly, two years later, Jennings had begun to tire of the outlaw obsession: in "Don't You Think This Outlaw Bit's Done Got Out of Hand?" he denounced the overexploitation and limitations of the repertoire designed only for "outlaw" performances.

The first song Willie Nelson, Kris Kristofferson, Waylon Jennings, and Johnny Cash recorded was Jimmy Webb's "The Highwayman," born of a vivid dream: "I had an old brace of pistols in my belt," says Webb, "and I was riding, hell-bent for leather . . . with sweat pouring off my body. I was terrified because I was being pursued by police, who were on the verge of shooting me. I sat up in bed. . . . Without even thinking about it, I stumbled out of bed to the piano . . . and within a couple of hours, I had the first verse" (Hutchinson, "Jimmy Webb's Story"). The song includes four verses, one for each artist, whose verse identifies him as a soul incarnate from the past, expressing continuity in this country's history, its people, and its greatness as a country. Webb says,

> I didn't know where the song was going. Then I realized that this guy doesn't really die in the first verse. He's reincarnated. I thought, "Where does this soul go?" The verses started to evolve. He becomes a sailor, then a dam builder. Then the best idea for me was switching the tense into the future and say, "I'll fly a starship across the universe divide until I reach the other side." (Hutchinson, "Jimmy Webb's Story")

Webb's song became a huge single hit that was then included in the first album, *Willie Nelson, Kris Kristofferson, Waylon Jennings and Johnny Cash* (1985) and was the opening song in every performance by the group. The group began using the name Highwaymen in 1990, after reaching an agreement with the original Highwaymen, a folk group of "Michael Row the Boat Ashore" fame. Willie Nelson sang, "I was a highwayman," followed by Kristofferson, whose first line is "I was a sailor"; and then Jennings, a dam builder; and finally Cash, who will "fly a starship across the universe divide."

At Nelson's Fourth of July annual picnic in 1985, the Highwaymen debuted before an immense gathering registering approval for their first album and soon went on the road. With a band composed of one musician from each artist's band, the group was welcomed to sellout

crowds. Onstage, the artists gave the appearance of enjoying the concert as they laughed and joked with each other. Kristofferson has said in
recollection that "he couldn't believe he was up there sharing the same
stage with them"; he was always in awe of Johnny Cash, remarking that
"he was always larger than life, and he always felt like something off
Mount Rushmore" (NPR staff).

"I don't think there are any other four people like us," says Jennings
in his autobiography. If we added one more, or replaced another, it
would never work. Nobody else was considered when the idea for a
group first started growing. There was never a fifth wheel." Jennings
speaks of their love for each other but says each worried about upstag-
ing the others. When they first went out together, Jennings declares, "it
looked like four shy rednecks trying to be nice to each other. It almost
ruined it. . . . After the opening night, I was fixin' to quit. I talked to
John about it and he was feeling the same way." Jennings believes we
"were boring each other and the audience," with their tiptoeing around
each other on stage. We decided to "poke some much-needed fun and
not take ourselves so danged serious" (342–44).

Of the songs in the first album (1985), with the exception of Jimmy
Webb's song "Highwayman," which is on the first track, all are covers,
and many deplore the passing of the old way of life and its values. "The
Last Cowboy Song," written by Ed Bruce and Ronald Peterson, essentially longs for the Old West and its values and, as the sad voices sing,
notes that "another piece of America's lost." In an impressive remem-
brance of the time of cowboys, each artist sings a verse chronicling
cowboy endeavors: Jennings sings of would-be cowboys, faced with en-
croaching civilization, yet dreaming of no fences; Kristofferson sings of
cowboys trailblazing with Lewis and Clark, facing down Wyatt Earp,
fighting bravely to the end at the Alamo with Colonel Travis, and going
down with General Custer and the Seventh Cavalry at Little Big Horn.
Nelson's verse pays tribute to Frederic Remington's pictures and paint-
ings of cowboys and their lifestyle and also Louis L'Amour's stories of
cowboys; Cash's spoken lyrics refer to the old Chisholm Trail now being
covered in concrete with traces of earlier activity of cowboys there
ignored. On a more personal level, the third song, "Jim, I Wore a Tie
Today," is about the loss of a friend of the narrators. Cash and Nelson
sing of his fever and their futile attempts to bring it down; they then
brought him into town for help but discovered "he was gone" when they

got there. When they saw he had been dressed up "in a fancy suit and tie" for his funeral, they dressed up too, each wearing a tie for the first time. Cash says he did not hear the preacher's words for remembering "back down the trail," to the good times they had when they were riding herd and panning for gold. The chorus repeats, "Oh, Jim, Jim, so you're riding on ahead . . . stake out a claim for me."

In "Desperados Waiting for a Train," Guy Clark, an admirer of Kristofferson, has written a soulful narrative song much like so many of Kristofferson's that depict characters who forge connections across generations. The song describes a man—seventy at the song's beginning—and the speaker, whose affection for each other lasted until the old man's death, which occurred about the time the speaker reached manhood. Five pictures of their relationship emerge during the song's progression: the speaker as a child going with the man to play dominoes with other men; the speaker playing "Red River Valley," as the man would sit in the kitchen and cry about the past; the speaker driving the man's car when the man was drunk; the speaker noting that the man, a former drifter and oil-well driller, was "one of the heroes of this country"; and the speaker visiting the old man the day before his death, when they closed their eyes and "dreamed us up a kitchen," singing another verse of "Red River Valley." Following each of the five verses, Clark repeats the chorus: "Like desperados waiting for a train." The song is autobiographical, and Clark has said this man was like a grandfather to him (Clark). This is the sixth track on the album.

"Welfare Line," the eighth track, written by Paul Kennerley, one-time husband of country singer Emmylou Harris, features three characters telling of their varied adventures in the past in direct contrast to his life at the present time. He had worked in steel; had fought for his country, winning a medal; and had "served on a Georgia road gang" because he could not pay his debts. He also remembers Rachel, who was "laid in a pauper's grave." In the chorus, the individual encourages his friends to pass the bottle around and "talk about the old times," because "night's rolling in" and it is cold on the welfare line. The song seems to follow the general pattern of songs in the supergroup's album, wherein the past posits a time of happiness or pleasant contentment compared to the loss of that happiness in current times.

One of Johnny Cash's songs, "Big River," observes, despite its lyrics, an upbeat tempo in an album of largely slower songs. One of Cash's early songs, written in 1958, and the fourth track, "Big River" relates the efforts of a man to keep up with a woman who avoids him in her travels down the Mississippi River. The speaker "met her accidentally in St. Paul, Minnesota" and has pursued her at length downstream to discover at various points that he has just missed her; growing weary of the pursuit in Memphis, he was overcome by desperation in Natchez, and in New Orleans, forsakes further pursuit, stating, "She loves you, Big River, more than me."

Another Cash song, resurrected from an ancient folio of songs, "Committed to Parkview," is a fitting addition to the Highwaymen album of the celebration of experiences representative of Americans. The fifth track is concerned with insanity and mental illness, rare subjects to appear in country music, but a subject becoming individuals whose struggle for success has taken its toll. Parkview possibly refers to the psychiatric wing of Park View Hospital in Nashville and may have been visited by Johnny Cash when he was drying out. The song begins with references to the Nashville music scene: Cash sings of a man who is convinced he is Hank Williams and is singing Williams's songs, and "a girl in 203" who is preoccupied with becoming a star and with the songs that she is convinced are quite good. Other patients in the hospital include "a girl in 307 coming down on Thorazine"; "a super star's ex-drummer trying to kick Benzedrine"; the son of a celebrity whose mother brought him to the hospital, because his dad is never home; several prosperous individuals who have "withdrawn from the rat race"; a woman who cries loudly enough "to wake the dead"; and "a singer who . . . attempted suicide." The song ends with Nelson and Cash relating the circumstances of their stay in Parkview: They are awakened early, and their blood pressure is monitored; they are asked how they feel. Johnny says, "Fantastic! There ain't nothing wrong with me," while Nelson is given an injection and goes right back to sleep. Johnny says ironically, "They're taking good care of me."

The seventh track on *The Highwaymen* is sung by Cash, Nelson, and Kristofferson, with Johnny Rodriguez—the only guest singer on the album. Written by Woody Guthrie and set to music by Martin Hoffman, a schoolteacher, the song, "Plane Wreck at Los Gatos," also known as "Deportee," is a protest song of the racist mistreatment of the Mexican farm workers, who, during their deportation, were killed in a plane crash on January 29, 1948. Guthrie was shocked by radio reports of the accident that gave no names of the victims, referring to them as "just deportees."

The ninth track, "Against the Wind," originally written and performed by Bob Seger in 1980, is sung by Jennings, Cash, and Nelson. In *The Highwaymen* version, Jennings sings the first verse about youth and its belief it can accomplish anything. The verse details the romance of the narrator and the "queen of our nights"; their passion was "like a wild fire out of control," with "nothing left to burn." Although they were young and strong, they "were running against the wind." The second verse, sung by Nelson, concerns the narrator later in his life, where he ran from things as long as he could and now needs "shelter against the wind." Cash's final lines in the song begin with, "All those drifter's days are past me now," and he sings of deadlines and commitment. All three join in the final chorus "Against the wind."

The tenth song, "The Twentieth Century Is Almost Over," by Steve Goodman and John Prine, features Willie Nelson and Johnny Cash, who recall prominent events such as World War II and the Great Depression, as well as notable inventions, and end with citing Father Time and Judgment Day.

On this album and also the second, the supergroup was credited "Nelson, Jennings, Cash, Kristofferson "; they were named "The Highwaymen" on the third album. This first album, however, was immensely popular and gave rise to concerts in huge venues around the world.

In the same year that this monumental album was released, 1985, a film featuring Kristofferson as lead actor and composer of the title song made its appearance. *Trouble in Mind* was directed by Alan Rudolph, an idiosyncratic director who wanted Kristofferson for his highly stylized film about an ex-cop just released from prison who gets involved with a young family new to the city. The song "The Hawk, or El Gavilan," the name of his character, is sung by Marianne Faithfull in the film and is also included in *Repossessed* (1986), the first album recorded by Kristofferson since 1981.

In 1990, the supergroup recorded their second album of ten songs, and of those, six were written by members of the group. The first one, "Silver Stallion," written by Lee Clayton, holds out the tantalizing myth of the cowboy on his silver stallion; he finds a "reckless woman," with "just a touch of sadness in her fingers," and they "ride like the one-eyed jack of diamonds / with the devil close behind." Kristofferson, Jennings,

and Nelson each sing a verse with Cash, and the backup singers combine their voices on the chorus. The second recorded song, "Born and
Raised in Black and White," written by Don Cook and John Harvis, and
performed by the entire group, is a simple view of people raised in
Texas. There is a strict dichotomy: some have books and others have
guns; one who became a gospel preacher, and one who had no plans,
but who liked the feel of a gun in his hand; and in the final verse, all sing
with the backup singers: "I chose the dark, you chased the light." "Two
Stories Wide," by Texan Willie Nelson, seems a good song to follow
"Born and Raised in Black and White," in its philosophical view of life.
It urges listeners to avoid extreme positions, seeking rather the middle.
"Come out of the darkness," Nelson's song states, "Come out in the
sunshine / and we'll be all right." While hiding in the night is to be
avoided, so is worrying and crying, because life is not only immeasur-
ably deep, it is "two stories wide." The song continues, insisting that
choosing a correct side is of no importance, for it is lonely on either
side, and "both sides . . . make your heart bleed." Following an instrumental break, Nelson repeats the line "Life's . . . two stories wide."

Similar to Jimmy Webb's "The Highwayman" in the first album is
"American Remains," written by Rivers Rutherford, in that it is about
"heroes of the homeland" who "live in many faces and answer many
names." Unlike the four incarnations of a single soul, Rutherford's song
details four archetypal Americans who were wounded but will "ride
again." Johnny Cash is the first singer, a guard who rides shotgun on a
passenger coach in Texas and is shot by a bandit; he vows, though
wounded, that "they'll never get the best of better men." Waylon Jennings is the character of a riverboat gambler out of New Orleans, who is
thrown overboard when an ace was dislodged from his sleeve. He vows
he did not cheat, and he'll ride again. Willie Nelson sings of being a
farmer in the Midwest who uses a John Deere tractor to make a living.
But the drought is killing his crops, and the bank is threatening foreclo-
sure. Of the "bank man," who claims to like him, Nelson sings, "he ain't
my friend." Kristofferson, as a Cherokee Indian, laments the white
man's abuse of the natural world and his attempt at poisoning the Native American's very existence. Kristofferson sings, "Nature is our mother / We are sucklings at her breast," as he vows to ride again. All four
artists join in the chorus that repeats, "Our memories live on in mortal
minds and poets' pens." They reiterate they'll "ride again." Rutherford,

the composer, had leapt over the property fence of producer Chips Moman, encountering barking dogs and security police, to deliver his demo to Moman—much the same as when Kristofferson had landed a helicopter on Cash's property. Moman was so impressed with this song that he made arrangements to include it in this album; Rutherford also plays guitar and sings backup vocals.

Kristofferson's song "Living Legend," sung by all the Highwaymen, looks back at historic events and asks of listeners their view of them today. This first appears to refer to this country's beginning and its early struggles. Willie Nelson sings, asking if they were better men than they'd ever been before. He then wonders if they would do the same today. "We were simple men," sings Kristofferson, thinking about the days when the dream of this country was born. "And we were smaller than you see." The second verse shifts in time to two thousand years ago: suggesting the crucifixion of Jesus Christ, Kristofferson asks, "Was he done in by the law?" Cash wonders what it was like then, "with our backs against the wall?" Kristofferson ponders the response if the same situation occurred today, "Would you still answer to the call? He ends the song asking, "Don't it matter anymore?" In his second song on the album, "Anthem 84," Kristofferson appears to answer the previous song's questions; he is disappointed in the U.S. government's actions, but he will not cease to believe in America.

Near the end of the album, Johnny Cash's song, "Songs That Make a Difference," performed by all four Highwaymen, refers to a legendary guitar pull at Cash's house that was almost unbelievably participated in by Bob Dylan, Shel Silverstein, Joni Mitchell, Graham Nash, Joe South, Roy Orbison, Eddie Rabbitt, Mickey Newbery, Johnny Cash, and Kristofferson. The two Highwaymen present at that event remember it as a magical night with some performers overcome with emotion and shedding tears; in the song, Nelson and Jennings attest to the fact that they would be content with menial work under stressful conditions if they could just sing along with songs like those that were sung that night. Left unsaid in Cash's song is the praise for songwriting as, at guitar pulls, singers sing their own songs. Cash and Kristofferson insist that they all can still sing songs that make a difference, if they follow the formula and "keep it from the heart and down to earth."

The second Highwaymen tour, promoting their second album, began with an opening show in Houston, Texas, traveling afterward to Las

Vegas for a week and heading back to Texas for Willie Nelson's Fourth of July Picnic. Following those festivities, the supergroup embarked for Australia and New Zealand and huge virtually sold-out venues.

Kristofferson continued acting in films in the early 1990s, but when not touring with the Highwaymen, he occasionally appeared at political rallies, once speaking for maverick Ross Perot's Reform Party as one of many Americans preferring a mainstream alternative. In October 1992, Kristofferson was invited to join a thirty-year celebration of Bob Dylan as a recording artist. As Dylan's "I'll Be Your Baby Tonight," one of Kristofferson's favorites, had been mentioned by Kristofferson as possibly having furnished a germ of the idea for "Help Me Make It through the Night," he was pleased to sing that song in Dylan's honor. All the songs performed during the celebration were recorded and marketed as a live, double-album *Bob Dylan's 30th Anniversary Concert Celebration*. On this same night, Irish singer Sinead O'Connor, who had recently appeared on *Saturday Night Live* and had torn up a picture of the pope, was introduced to the audience at Madison Square Garden, whereupon she was promptly booed by some of the audience. Terrified, O'Connor ran into the arms of Kristofferson, who had just been instructed by a stage manager to get her off the stage. "I wasn't about to tell her to get off the stage so I walked out and said to her, 'Don't let the bastards get you down,' and she said 'I'm not down.' On an interview on Ireland's National Television and Radio Broadcasting, he spoke of O'Connor as a very courageous person who had been misunderstood" (Kristofferson, O'Callaghan interview).

In 1995, the Highwaymen set about their third and final album, *The Road Leads on Forever*. It was recorded in California and produced by Don Was, credited with the ability to renew artists' careers that had become inert. Despite the fact that all four members of the aging supergroup were fading in the competition with the current brand of country singers, and benefitted hugely from the success of the Highwaymen, Kristofferson may well have benefitted most of all. With the decline in his recording sales of the last two albums in his contract, he had given up attempting to record solo albums, relying only on collaborations, such as the Highwaymen, which apparently convinced Mercury to offer him a contract soon after their first album. Kristofferson recorded two albums, *Repossessed* (1985) and *Third World Warrior* (1990), that contained songs with political themes and protests against the U.S. government's manipulations in Central America. The first album was received quite well, but the second, an angry and bitter criticism of the government, was a commercial disaster. Since that time, his recording career had been in hiatus, with no new albums.

The third album for the Highwaymen was Kristofferson's favorite; he appreciated the studio feel to it as opposed to the live performances of the earlier two albums. Not as rough about the edges as some of the earlier songs, these utilized some of Los Angeles's prime studio musicians, who backed four songs written by the Highwaymen themselves, and others by outlaws of various sorts. The first song was "The Devil's Right Hand," a murder ballad written by Steve Earle, and previously recorded by Waylon Jennings, that lends authenticity to the outlaw legend. Plainly showing the allure of a gun, the song shows the responsibility for one's conduct despite the speaker's final insistence on his own innocence: "Nothing touched the trigger but the devil's right hand."

Interestingly enough, Jennings's contribution, the number 5 track on the album, is a plaintive statement of his faith, which, by his own admission, "has never been that strong." He sings, "I don't talk too much about it," but believes "that I should live life at its fullest." Willie Nelson, in a less spiritual vein, sings that he is reaching the end of understanding someone who has hurt him, and Johnny Cash sings a bizarre song, "Death and Hell," with thoughts of the dark side. The number 10 track is Kristofferson's song "Here Comes That Rainbow Again," written with John Steinbeck's *Grapes of Wrath* or perhaps John Ford's film version in mind. In the story, the younger Joad children, on their Okie family trek to California during the Great Depression, enter a gas station in search of a stick of candy; realizing they are short of enough money, the kind owner gives them the candy anyway, a move spotted by a customer, who returns the favor with an unusually large tip.

"True Love Travels a Gravel Road," by Dallas Frazier and A. L. Owens, epitomizes the kind of steadfastness outlaws desire in mates, specifically in choosing love over money. Each Highwaymen sings a verse extolling the love that grows stronger over hard or lean times: Willie Nelson wonders "how many hearts could face the winters we've known / and still not turn cold"; and Waylon Jennings notes, "Not once have I seen your blue eyes fill with envy." Billy Joe Shaver and his son, Eddy, are the writers of "Live Forever," an unusual song about fame;

occupying the second track on the album, the speaker proclaims he will live forever, "just like the songs I leave behind me." Jennings sings a verse exhorting parents to "raise your children right," and Cash adds, "Don't let the darkness take them" but instead lead them into the light.

Following two songs, "Everybody Gets Crazy" and "It Is What It Is," that testify to the common vicissitudes in the lives of the Highwaymen and their listeners, the four sing "The Road Goes On Forever," a song by Robert Earle Keen Jr., which brings the album to a close. A long ballad of doomed love that could have almost been written by Kristofferson, the song chronicles the story of Sherry, a waitress, and Sonny, a loner, who delivered Sherry from a groping drunk with his pool cue. Sherry and Sonny jumped into his pickup truck and drove to Miami Beach. There, the money ran out, and in attempting a deal with some Cubans, they were surprised by lawmen, whereupon Sherry rescued Sonny by shooting an officer. Giving her the money, Sonny tells her to "say I forced you into this," and he drove away. Twenty-one months later, Sherry returns to town—the day the headlines tell the world that Sonny is going to the chair—driving "her new Mercedes Benz." All the Highwaymen repeat the chorus: "The road goes on forever / and the party never ends," implying that the Highwaymen and their concerts, much like the events in the song, will result in continued echoing in the future.

In 1995, the Highwaymen gave up their touring and traveling, with each one returning to his own career. They all benefitted from their years together as a group, and when the final album, thought by many to be the best of the three, failed to meet their expectations, they signed off on the effort. But Kristofferson was to benefit later on from his association with Don Was, producer of *The Road Goes On Forever*.

6

"I DON'T BELIEVE THAT NO ONE WANTS TO KNOW"

1985–1991

When he was eight years old, Kristofferson and his mother went into Brownsville to celebrate the homecoming of a World War II Brownsville native, a Hispanic soldier who had been awarded the Congressional Medal of Honor for his distinguished service in the European theater of war. They were shocked to discover they were the only two Anglos present at an event that would ordinarily inspire an entire town with pride. His mother's ire regarding the prejudice displayed by her fellow Brownsville Anglo citizens never left him; in fact, it generated a strong sense of right and wrong that remained with him throughout his entire life. While likely linked to her military zeal, his mother's response came from a robust sense of duty to God and country united with a sturdy ethic involving moral duty and obligation. Kristofferson was taught the importance of his country in his life and his duty to uphold its honor and purpose. All of this had made his yearning to become a songwriter wrenching and had made it an agonizing experience to learn about the U.S. government's misrepresentations regarding its intentions in Vietnam. It also meant that his responses to the government's deception would be guided by the memory of his mother's remarks.

In 1965, when his three tours of duty in Germany were up, and he was in search of a life purpose, he volunteered for Vietnam but was turned down because of an impending assignment to teach at West

Point. At that juncture, he resigned his commission and, in a complete about-face, had begun to pursue a career in songwriting; this shocking behavior had actually represented a desperate attempt to live his own life, but to his stunned family it constituted a total rejection of their values and was followed swiftly by their essential disowning of him. Still, while the abandonment by his family cut deeply, he continued to be very proud of their service to their country and to have faith in the principles on which America was founded. "I believed we were fighting for freedom" in Vietnam, he declared (Jordan).

But, the farther he got from the army, the more he began to reconsider. During his stay in West Germany, Kristofferson had witnessed career officers returning from Vietnam who reported events that had sickened them to the core and, as a result, had left the army. In the Gulf of Mexico, while flying helicopters to offshore rigs, he spoke with numerous fighter pilots back from Vietnam with chilling stories to tell. In 1969, the My Lai massacre of hundreds of unarmed South Vietnamese civilians, including mostly women, children, and elderly persons, became public. After much reflection and the discovery of additional information, Kristofferson became aware of the situation in Vietnam to a shocking degree. "As you start being exposed to things like this, the more you examine it, the worse it is, and the more you find out about things like the Phoenix Project, where we killed between 30,000 and 60,000 civilians, and you find out the CIA in Laos killed 100,000 civilians, and that we were involved in the drug trade," he said. "The more I read, the more I realized that our government may *never* have stood for the things I believe in" (Jordan). He then became engaged in a "steady process—sort of having scales cleaned off your eyes—to the point that you have to get used to a whole new perception of what it is that your country stands for. For a kid who grew up in Brownsville, Texas, God was on our side and our country stood for justice. It was very disturbing" (Jordan). He reached the conclusion that "we killed 2,000,000 Vietnamese, 56,000 American soldiers, and we killed the notion for a lot of Americans that America stands for liberty and justice for everybody" (Pinkston).

Later, he shrank in disbelief that he had been so slow to learn the truth; because he came from a military family, he believed what he had read in the *Stars and the Stripes* and heard through military channels. The truth about America's role in Vietnam was a bitter pill to swallow and spurred him to speak out regarding his political views. Early in his performing career, Kristofferson had begun supporting Caesar Chavez and the United Farm Workers, his concerts also including frequent benefits that endorsed the causes of human rights, Native Americans, and peace and environmental concerns. But his growing disillusionment led him to incorporate progressive and antiwar lyrics, as well as sharp rhetoric concerning human rights. Like many other Americans jolted by the reality of the Vietnam conflict, he grew to mistrust all institutions, placing instead a high premium on his own personal freedom. Long-held political beliefs had no place in his life any longer; he was becoming a left-wing activist.

By 1979, Kristofferson became aware of the Sandinista revolution in Nicaragua, which overthrew a brutal dictatorship supported by the United States; and by the mid-eighties, he grew weary of the Reagan administration's military intervention aimed at illegally arming and training Contra revolutionaries invested in subverting the elected administration. Perceiving the U.S. government's use of the "Communist threat" to justify engaging in a war against the freedom- seeking Nicaraguans, he sensed a repetition of the misinformation about the circumstances in Vietnam. Exercising his still bristling sense of right and wrong, he took action; and using his songwriting talents, he combined his convictions with his art and began to do what he had always done best—write songs.

In 1986, Kristofferson recorded *Repossessed* for Mercury Records, as part of a contract extended to him most likely on the strength of his affiliation with the Highwaymen, whose profit from the eponymous album the previous year was huge. The politically turbulent period of 1986–1987 provoked several liberal songwriters, including Jackson Browne, who remembered the U.S. government's equivocation concerning Vietnam and saw Nicaragua as the U.S. government's most recent target in its war on "political instability" in Latin America. The title, *Repossessed*, suggested by Kristofferson's longtime guitarist and friend Stephen Bruton, conjured up a double meaning in its reference to the Kristofferson recording that was intended to follow *To the Bone* (1980) but vanished in Monument Records' bankruptcy, and also to his revived political passion. His first solo album in over six years boasts the Borderlords as his backup band and singers, which included good friends Bruton and Billy Swan doing double duty on guitar and vocals,

Donnie Fritts on keyboards and vocals, and Glen Clark's guitar, harmonica, keyboards, and vocals. Possibly the best-known composition on the album is "They Killed Him," a song written in memoriam to Kristofferson's martyred heroes, Mahatma Gandhi, Martin Luther King Jr., and Jesus Christ. Covered by Bob Dylan later on that same year, the song followed the efforts of the three "holy" men against injustice and the price they paid for those efforts. Of Gandhi, Kristofferson says, "He would not bow down, he would not fight" his oppressors and became "just another holy man who tried to make a stand." Martin Luther King "shook the land like rolling thunder / and made the bells of freedom ring today," but he "dared to be a friend," and "they killed him!" As for "the holy one called Jesus Christ," who "healed the lame and fed the hungry / and for his love they took his life away," Kristofferson notes his fate was the result, then as now, of being "just the holy son of man we'll never understand."

Riled by the dissembling of the country that he, his family, and innumerable others had offered their lives to defend as a beacon of truth and justice to the world, he included in this album various expressions of his bitterness. "Shipwrecked in the Eighties" laments the plight of Vietnam veterans who, "lost and alone in deep water," were still adrift and going "farther away from the shore." Feeling cut off, ignored, or forgotten by the United States after their service and sacrifice, the veterans in Kristofferson's song also suffer from feelings of betrayal by the country they loved. "When they prove something wrong you believed in so long you go crazy," intimates a loss of faith in their country, while the cry, "Holy Toledo! I can't see the light any more / All those horizons I used to guide me are gone," expresses feelings of being utterly lost following their experiences in Vietnam.

Sadness and regret seem to prompt "Anthem 84," a look at America's loss of integrity. "You were such a pretty dream as I remember," says the speaker, remembering the United States as she had been when she was "young and strong and God was on your side." But then, the "vision slowly faded," and "you traded your compassion for your pride." Despite his dismay, he will not abandon hope for his country. Declaring "I ain't going to leave you for the crazy things you're doing," he vows to fight to defend and love America, because "I still believe in all that we believed in."

"What About Me?" is a bitter song that links Vietnam and Central America in its indictment of the U.S. government's duplicitous involvement in those areas. The wasted soldier's stabbing query, "Do you believe in freedom?" while signaling the disaster of the Vietnam conflict, mocks President Reagan's easy litanies on democracy that concealed his support of an authoritarian regime. In the chorus, a connection is established between the soldier and the child of murdered Sandinista parents: to the question, "Do you believe in freedom?" the speaker answers, "I do"; then the rejoinder, "Oh! What about me?" rings in the air.

"El Gavilan" (The Hawk), sung by Marianne Faithfull in the Alan Rudolph film *Trouble in Mind* (1985) and included in the album, reminds listeners that "you gotta make your own rules, child / You gotta break your own chains"; "El Coyote" observes that "lonesome coyotes survive"; this autobiographical reference to Kristofferson and his cubs (children) repeats that a part of him will always be wild, and all he can "leave them is love and a reason / to run for the rest of their lives." Despite the anger that characterizes much of the album, songs of love and philosophical statements are there also: "The heart is all that matters in the end," from "The Heart," is a tribute to his father, whose "spirit fills my body like a song"; and in "Love Is the Way," previously recorded by Johnny Cash and Waylon Jennings on their album *Heroes*, Kristofferson warns against "killing each other," as encouraged by the "gospel of hate."

The music world was surprised by this new kind of music issuing from Kristofferson, certainly like no other he had recorded. Hearing the anger in the songs, listeners considered them political songs, whereupon Kristofferson declared he did not see them as such: they were "songs about what is going on in the world" (Miller, 188). The album was quite popular, with "They Killed Him" having a great deal to do with that, and it was promoted aggressively by Kristofferson who acquainted concertgoers with the songs and backgrounds, and provided specific commentary.

In 1987, Kristofferson appeared in *Amerika*, a fourteen-hour miniseries on ABC that created a furor of controversy. A paranoid fantasy premised on the Nazis winning World War II, the film depicts life in America in 1997, ten years following its takeover by Russia in a bloodless coup. Kristofferson stars as the U.S. resistance leader and former maverick presidential candidate, who ran for office after the takeover began (and has been imprisoned). Sam Neill plays the KGB administrator. Running over seven nights, the miniseries kindled inordinate consternation for a number of people, including Kristofferson who, having endured the venom of the more conservative element for years, now, for his part in the film, was being furiously attacked by the left who despised his presumed rightist agenda. What *Amerika* actually accomplished for him, however, was to help him focus his political ideas: "At that time I was trying to find a way to be active about policy in Central America and didn't have a clue where to start" (Jordan).

The belief that freedom carries with it the obligation to protect that freedom motivated Kristofferson to extend his efforts toward that end. Beyond initiating a number of human rights concerts, he sang at a human rights concert in Mexico, there meeting up with the members of a Nicaraguan band and Carlos Mejia Godoy, an outstanding songwriter. Associated with the Sandinista movement, Godoy had recorded albums containing popular anthems for workers and revolutionaries, featured later in compilation albums, *Nicaraguan Revolution*, volumes 1 and 2. Kristofferson gradually become involved in peace talks, ironically attending one such conference in Russia at the time of *Amerika*'s release (and igniting some far-right complaints that he had intentionally sabotaged the film's message by participating in the peace meeting). Part of a three-day peace forum in Moscow during the Mikhail Gorbachev regime, he was a member of a delegation from the Internal Center for Development Policy based in Washington, D.C., that included Norman Mailer, Gore Vidal, and recently released dissident Andrei Sakharov. Kristofferson and his fellow panelists received considerable criticism for their appearance, seen as lending support to the Communist regime.

In 1988, he met Brian Willson, a former Vietnam officer turned political activist, who in 1987, along with two other protesters against U.S. policy in Central America, sat on a train track in Concord, California, to block a shipment of ammunition headed for Nicaragua. Expecting to be arrested and probably fined, the three, in a well-planned and publicized nonviolent protest, planned to call attention to the huge munitions shipments that exited the Concord Naval Weapons Station and traveled on flatbed trains down the three-mile track to the ship waiting on the Sacramento River to begin the final leg of their journey to Nicaragua. There, the weapons would be used to kill or maim those whom President Reagan and the U.S. government deemed as opponents of the Contras. The train usually stopped for anything on the track, but the train crew, stunned by their explicit orders not to stop, actually sped up, running over Willson (the other two protesters managed to jump free of the track in time), severing his legs, crushing part of his skull, and breaking a total of nineteen bones in his body. After several brain surgeries, in the following spring Willson and Kristofferson traveled to Nicaragua at the invitation of President Daniel Ortega, where Willson received a hero's welcome and was driven, with Kristofferson in the back seat, through the streets of Managua as Nicaraguans shouted his name. Willson remembers Ortega driving slowly as people reached in and touched his arm shouting, "Brian, Brian!" He said, "Kris, who as a successful singer-songwriter knew how it felt to be famous, tapped me on the shoulder from behind and asked, 'How are you dealing with this?'" Willson was too overwhelmed to say (Willson, 253–54). The following day, Kristofferson, Willson, and their entourage traveled to Sapoa, eighty miles south of Managua, to observe the first "peace" talks between the Contras and Sandinistas. Willson speaks of how the road to their destination was lined with cheering peasants desperate for peace. From Sapoa, the trip continued for about ten days in all; the group visited Sandinista combat troops, met with U.S. officials, and possibly marked Kristofferson's first visit to the injured in several hospitals (254).

Kristofferson and Willson surely compared the similarity of their youthful devotion to the myth of America and its nobility, and their eagerness to defend their country, only to discover the lies that had been propagated to disguise its true intent. Both suspected the worst about Vietnam, and later investigations proved they were correct; each was devastated by learning the truth about Vietnam and subsequently encountered difficulty in following orders, or automatically respecting any authority figure again. Both were distressed by the ideology of American superiority used to condition children in a comfortable belief system preventing them even as adults from any recognition (unless, of course, they experience troubling events such as those occurring in Vietnam, Central America, or many other places around the world) that America is not the shining beacon of truth and justice they had believed.

His concern for events in Nicaragua had led to an invitation to visit the country and see firsthand what was happening there. He ended up

going down two or three times . . . to—four times, maybe—visit the
hospitals full of kids [who] had their legs and arms blown off by the
mines we were putting in and finding out that the Contras that we
were training, the terrorists that we were sending down there were
not attacking the Sandinista Army but were attacking the so-called
soft targets—the schools, the health facilities, and the agricultural co-
ops. And it will radicalize you. (Kristofferson, Paulson interview, 6)

In the interview with Kristofferson in 1991, Rosa Jordan prefaced it
by pondering how he had kept going while under attack from both left
and right, and how he had avoided the burnout so many activists suffer.
She remembered meeting him at a Gulf War protest involving a sym-
bolic spill of blood and ashes; he anticipated arrest, but only Martin
Sheen and activist Valerie Sklarevsky were taken. But mostly she wonders, "How does he—how does anybody—get from a US Army captain
who volunteered for Vietnam to this man on his knees in public opposition to the blood being spilled in the Persian Gulf and Central America?" (Jordan).

The answer to Jordan's question lay in the weight of Kristofferson's
own personal knowledge of the devastation (much like Willson's witnessing of the wanton bombing of the Vietnamese villagers initiated a
change in his own consciousness) noted in his statements above and
again below:

I think it's like the priests who get radicalized by their experience. I
was brought in close contact (with the situation in Central America)
by a woman from El Salvador who was helping me raise my daughter
when I was a single father after I got divorced. This woman had a
family she was supporting back home that was devastated by the
death squads. While she was working for me, they were looking for
her brother, who was a college student and therefore, according to
the government we support, a Communist. They took his sister's
three-month-old baby and . . . killed the baby right in front of her.
The more I learned about what we were doing down there, the more
horrible it seemed. (Jordan)

In 1989, Kristofferson played the part of an American journalist in
the film *Sandino*, made in Nicaragua and directed by prominent exiled
Chilean director Michael Littin. The story told of the heroic feats of
General August C. Sandino, who, with his ragged band of rebels, re-

pulsed the 1927 attempt of the U.S. government to take over Nicaragua. Sandino was murdered in 1934 by the opposition and became a national hero, lending his name to the Sandinistas, who were targeted in the 1980s by the Reagan-supported Contras. Kristofferson observed that "it was very interesting, making a film about Sandino fighting against the Marines at the same time the Sandinistas were fighting against American mercenaries" (Jordan).

On one of his trips to Nicaragua, Kristofferson saw Eugene Hasenfus, the American cargo handler and only survivor in a Contra supply plane shot down by the Sandinistas. Feeling more sympathetic toward the Sandinistas than toward the Americans who attempted to overthrow their duly elected government, Kristofferson visited Hasenfus nevertheless. He said,

> They asked me if I wanted to meet him and I thought, well, he is an American, maybe I could give him some hope. . . . I told him, "But for a couple of twists that happened along in my life, I could be in the same position you're in." He was just a guy who believed what they told him. They had told him he was fighting for his country, which was, you know, fighting Communism. I had volunteered to go to Vietnam to do the same thing. (Jordan)

In 1990, he released a second album, *Third World Warrior*, also for Mercury Records, that contained grim depictions of the inhumanity of the Contras in their assaults on the innocent. Kristofferson said,

> The record company printed a minimum number of copies and dropped me off their label, and there weren't many reviews. One running in the *USA Today* did write it was good to see something out of a country songwriter that wasn't right-wing hogwash. I think maybe a lot of reviewers . . . don't know how to deal with an album like that. I was just gratified that the musicians I respect like it and say it's good music. (Jordan)

Understandably, no stations would play the records; actually, the studio did not even market the album. Kristofferson continued performing the songs in concert to mixed reactions: toward songs concerning the U.S. government's policy and situation in Central America, some members of the audience would express their distaste; other concertgoers vowed to look at the matter further. More conservative audiences also had mixed reactions, some in states of disbelief rejected his account of the situation totally; others were angry. Once when he sang "Don't Let the Bastards Get You Down," the line "They're killing babies in the name of freedom" elicited an infuriated outburst from one follower: "I'll never listen to another song you write." Kristofferson inquired whether the source of her distress was the song or the fact that the United States was responsible for the actions, but he received no answer (Kristofferson, Paulson interview, 7). In Atlanta, during the Oliver North trial, his political comments prompted about three hundred out of two thousand concertgoers to ask for their money back.

Also in 1990, Kristofferson and the Highwaymen had recorded their second album, *The Highwaymen II*, at Columbia, which was released one week before *Third World Warrior*. The album includes "Anthem 84," from *Repossessed*, whose performance on the nearly sold-out second Highwaymen tour occasionally included Kristofferson's political comments. The ethos of *The Highwayman II* and *Third World Warrior* is seemingly so contrary as to cause the coexistence of the two to be unlikely. Yet, the concern Kristofferson had for the human beings he felt had been misused by his own government clearly had no conflict with the love and esteem he bore his friends and the music they played and sang together. Dissension ensued among certain members of the band and crew accompanying the Highwaymen who, during Kristofferson's remarks, reputedly held up signs that read, "THAT DOESN'T GO FOR ME" (Miller, 203). Also, rumors of Waylon Jennings's disenchantment with the situation flew thick and fast. Stacy Harris, Nashville journalist, recalls interviewing Kristofferson, who related at some length his opinions and the reasons he felt he should be writing and promoting political songs. Afterward, she was stopped by Jennings, who complained that she asked Kristofferson about politics, saying, "We've been trying to get him to shut up about that stuff." Jennings feared Kristofferson's records and political statements would be bad publicity for the band (Miller, 203–4). However, Johnny Cash, who had long maintained sympathy for the American Indians, was tolerant of Kristofferson's liberal rants and activist efforts, and was also a strong supporter of Kristofferson's right to express his opinions. Cash went so far as to write to *Country Music* defending Kristofferson and reminding the publication's readers that, unlike some of his critics, he had served in the U.S. Army (Miller, 204). Through it all, Willie Nelson was unflappable.

But the Highwaymen were not altogether typical of country music writers, singers, musicians, or followers; if not outright Democrats, the four were liberal thinkers in a traditionally conservative community whose sharp response to Kristofferson's perceived "hippie" ideas and behavior more than twenty years earlier was equally harsh with regard to his political songs. As Bill Malone, country music historian, notes, "In previous decades, while patriotism, a populist voice, and support for the armed forces remain common themes, partisan politics are mostly absent from mainstream, commercial country music." Malone points out,

> In 2004, organizers at the Republican National Convention planned a tribute to the recently deceased Johnny Cash, which promptly sparked a protest from Cash fans who were certain that the singer's politics fell along Democratic lines. While both sides of the political spectrum were attempting to claim the singer, Cash's estate released a statement that carefully avoided aligning him with either. As many industry insiders have observed, when one's livelihood depends directly on fans, it is just smart business strategy not to advertise one's political affiliation lest it alienate any potential record buyers. (478–79)

Not only was *Third World Warrior* not marketed by Mercury Records, but also it disappeared. When producer Al Bunetta sought to rerelease it in 2003, he was told that it was gone. Eventually it was located and rereleased along with *Repossessed* in 2004 by Oh Boy Records, a small independent organization set up in 1984 by singer-songwriter John Prine, his manager Al Bunetta, and a friend, Dan Einstein. The album's later entrance into a world for which it was not intended, yet managing to achieve some small popularity, is not surprising; while its plea for the release of Nelson Mandela from prison was nullified as that occurred prior to the album's release, its primary reason for existence, the deplorable situation in Nicaragua, was relieved through the defeat of the Sandinistas through a national election also occurring before the album's release. Kristofferson said, "I think we . . . beat that revolution, not with the Contras and Oliver North, and all that, but with money. And we bought an election. . . . And the people voted with their stomachs, you know? They thought it was going to help them. Unfortunately, today, they're the second poorest country in the hemisphere" (Kristofferson, Paulson interview, 7).

Third World Warrior is a concept album containing ten topical political songs that relate specifically to Central America. All songs are
written by Kristofferson except one, for which he is cowriter, and all
songs exhibit rhythms contrary to traditional country music. The first
track, "The Eagle and the Bear," establishes the speaker's military
stance: he will fight and die for freedom "up against an eagle or a bear";
he will help his brother with no regard for those who might not approve
of his actions; he has served honorably in the army and has watched his
country "stagger like a dying man"; and he will not try to ignore it
anymore. He says, "I'll defend what I believe in in a land of Liberty /
like my father did before," and he will pray for El Salvador, Nicaragua,
and the release of Nelson Mandela from prison. To a background largely of piano and drums, Kristofferson delivers the song in a stalwart
manner with the drums contributing to a marching effect. The second
track, "Third World Warrior," in turn, introduces listeners to the soldier
fighting for freedom in Nicaragua and El Salvador: "You'll never beat
him with weapons and money." Loud electric guitars open the song and
propel country-rock through Kristofferson's descriptions of the soldier
and his ill treatment by the United States. His determination concludes
in the line, repeated like a mantra, "There ain't no chain as strong as the
will to be free."

Song 3, "Aguila Del Norte" (The Eagle of the North), as spoken by
Kristofferson, represents the American Eagle from the south-of-the-
border viewpoint, a comment that suggests, during his youth in
Brownsville, his awareness of the eagle's attitude of condescension toward Mexico, a country perceived as containing second-class, nonwhite
citizens. In Nicaragua, the eagle characterizes the "terror from above,"
as it reminds Central Americans of the U.S. government's decades-old
control of the area for its benefit. Nicaraguans are forced to vote for a
U.S. backed regime; if they rebel, they are crushed, but if they vote as
instructed, they merely starve. The song depicts the Contras striking
swiftly, wreaking havoc upon women and children; its menacing effects
are musically produced by electric guitars and synthesizers. Other individuals are seen "running from the shadows"; they mock the United
States' boastful display of its accomplishments. Kristofferson mocks
Reagan's democratic speeches by saying, "You believe in freedom, and
you believe in justice / but not in Nicaragua." In another verse, the

terrified people in Central America inquire of the United States, "What is in your heart?"

In the fourth song, "The Hero," Kristofferson asks listeners, "Would you like to be a hero in your life?" In a world so devoid of heroes, he suggests they might bring life to people deadened by the loss of hope brought about by oppression. He asks if they would like to trade places with Jesus on the cross, explaining that they can be as good as they want to be. He asks his audience to consider several individuals perceived as heroes and think of how they became heroes. His final inquiry concerns doing one's duty; and he believes that if one is bound to do one's duty then the time has come. The song seems to refer to speaking out concerning the U.S. intervention in Central America.

Song 5 uses as its title one of the more famous lines coming from World War II, "Don't Let the Bastards Get You Down." The first line, "They're killing babies in the name of freedom," references the deception connection between Vietnam and Central America, emphasized in the following line: "We've been down that sorry road before." Kristofferson declares it is no longer possible to fool those who know the truth. He laments the U.S. loss of vision resulting from the murders of heroes (John F. Kennedy, Martin Luther King Jr.) and notes the powerful and controlling U.S. government authorities, observing, "It's getting hard to listen to their lies." In the chorus, he remembers his father, wondering what he might think "if he'd seen the way they turned this dream around." He concludes that in consideration of the events engineered by the U.S. government regarding Central America, he says he must operate according to what his father told him: "Try to tell the truth / and stand your ground" and adds finally, "Don't let the bastards get you down."

"Love of Money," with a decidedly Latino beat, presents two situations in two countries: in the first, a woman runs "for the border and her life" and survives by selling herself, and "in the end all she had to sell them was her soul"; in the second, inhabitants were looking toward the future "in a land where everything was free" but "worldly men turned their profits into war." The last line, "No one knows who we're really fighting for," reflects the confusion regarding the real goals and reasons for fighting in Vietnam as well as in Central America and contends that the people of both countries had been sold out by leaders seeking profit.

In "Third World War," Kristofferson describes the Nicaraguan Revolution as "Where the young men's brave new visions / threaten old men's selfish dreams," and the old men, having no idea what to do, call the young men Communists. The old men, rich and powerful, have a clear advantage over their young opponents, for "the odds are never even / and their skins are never white." In this third world war, the rich get richer and the poor become their victims, but Kristofferson believes the young, poor man will win out "cause he's fighting for his future and / his freedom and his sons."

Song 8, "Jesse Jackson," sung with Willie Nelson, is Kristofferson's tribute to Jackson for his activism in Alabama, Cuba, and Nicaragua; his work with Martin Luther King Jr.; and his ideals, specifically his belief "in the better side of Human." Jackson was admired as a presidential candidate.

"Mal Sacate," with its arrangement and guitar accompaniment by T-Bone Burnett, is first a confrontation of "Mr. Money Man," concerning his stolen land and the murdered heroes whose dreams still remain. The chorus affirms the Hispanic saying that fire will not burn a bad weed, referring to the difficulty in killing the stubborn dreams of some of the murdered people; and similarly depicted in the saying, common in El Salvador, "a bad thing never dies." The final verse recounts the names of heroes who have been murdered.

"Sandinista," song 10, became a very controversial song as it is a tribute to the Sandinista movement, its values, and the truth and freedom it brings to the people of Nicaragua. Kristofferson sees its spirit holding a candle in the darkness, the "keeper of the flame."

While in Nashville in 2003, as part of a celebration of free speech, Kristofferson received the Spirit of Americana Award, presented by the Americana Music Association and the First Amendment Center. He also appeared on *Speaking Freely*, a weekly television show there, and spoke with Ken Paulson, who asked him if he thought his political music would make a difference in the world, to which Kristofferson answered, "I don't know. . . . All I knew is it was the only thing I could do to make a difference. . . . And it was coming from the heart." Paulson asks, "Do you think that your political stands hurt your career?" Kristofferson answers, "Who knows what hurts a career. . . . I remember, when I put out the *Third World Warrior*, I read one review, I think it was in *USA Today*. It said, "Surely he knows pigs will fly before they play this on the air." But I can't think . . . of anything I would have done differently" (Kristofferson, Paulson interview, 7).

Kristofferson's politically polarizing songs angered individuals in the opposition party, and he was deserted by droves of country music supporters. Despite the fact that he lost most of his traditional country music base, he began to regain many formerly alienated supporters as time passed. Following the Gulf War and the invasion of Iraq, many Americans viewed the U.S. government from a different perspective, and a number of disaffected music lovers began to review Kristofferson's outspokenness against some of its policies. Traditional country music fans were not among them, to be evidenced by the furor caused by the comment of Natalie Maines of the Dixie Chicks, concerning her embarrassment from being from the same state as President Bush.

Kristofferson's biographer, Stephen Miller, looks on his activism with disdain, deriding his being "fired up by the righteousness of his beliefs" and labeling his conviction that "he had a duty to tell people what was going on" as merely a "patronizing defence" (195). Miller went on to say,

> The emotion and subtlety that Kristofferson was able to express in his earlier love and relationship songs was eradicated by the grating anger of his delivery. . . . *Third World Warrior* was a series of preachy and simplistic political soundbites—in many ways similar to John Lennon's 1972 reportage journal, *Some Time in New York City*, which many considered damaging to Lennon's post-Beatles solo career. Kristofferson conceded as much when he said he would never play a concert that only included political material. (205)

Although the Sandinista distress in Nicaragua had been removed through the U.S.-engineered electoral process, Kristofferson's protests against injustice did not conclude; his songs shifted slightly from political agitation to the realm of human rights. The nearly extinct recording career he had left in 1979 and revisited briefly with his activist songs—a move thought by many to have killed it off for good—was probed and determined to be still breathing. He began working with Don Was, a noted producer and resuscitator of the foundering careers of musicians, many of whom, thanks to Was, had enjoyed revitalized second acts in their careers. Kristofferson recorded *A Moment of Forever*, from original songs, backed by an assortment of first-rate Los Angeles session musicians singularly appropriate for his renewed and more ambitious effort at being a singer-songwriter. The album, however, was a victim of a distribution deal gone bad, and it was shelved until 1995. Upon its release by the independent Justice label, it was met with enthusiastic reviews, applause, and acclaim.

The album of fourteen songs, some older and some more lyrical than others, continues, without explicit organization, to express Kristofferson's feelings about freedom and fighting against oppression. One, a rocking country song, condemns situations where people are being compelled to live under policies against their wishes; written earlier and inappropriately for *Songwriter*, "Under the Gun" was by that time already a preoccupation for Kristofferson. The land whose story is being told, presumably Nicaragua or El Salvador, has reached this point by way of "swollen men, blind with power," who, concerned only with themselves and the benefits to them, have made their games dangerous for all who live there. In breaking all the rules, the ruthless men break men, promises, hearts, and homes. More importantly, the children, hungry and wild, who are "born under the gun" will die "reaching for freedom." Kristofferson welcomes the opportunity to speak out about the situation in Central America and believes the truth should be held "like a candle" and allowed to shine "like the sun" on any love that remains "in a world under the gun."

"Johnny Lobo," Kristofferson's tribute to John Trudell, whose activism against the U.S. government's policies regarding Native Americans resulted in tragedy, amounts to an assault upon the government's refusal to compromise. Reared on the Santee Reservation in northern Nebraska, Trudell served in the U.S. Navy, attended college, and in 1969, became deeply involved with Indians of All Tribes and the takeover at Alcatraz. He later became the national chairman for the American Indian Movement, and in 1979, while he was in Washington, D.C., the home of his wife's parents on Duck Valley Indian Reservation in Nevada suspiciously burned, killing his pregnant wife, their three children, and his wife's mother. Kristofferson's song follows Johnny from his early life on the reservation dreaming of open spaces while being "locked inside a heaven gone to hell," yet following the rules and growing into a warrior "fighting for his people and his soul." Much later, weary of a history of failed attempts at communication with the U.S. government, Johnny "burned a flag he knew had been dishonored"; afterward, his

house was burned. Kristofferson's lyrics, however, achieve a more positive tone than those in Peter La Farge's "Ballad of Ira Hayes," a story of
the Native American Marine who was one of the six soldiers photographed in 1945 by AP photographer Joe Rosenthal while raising the
American flag on Mount Suribachi, Iwo Jima; in the song, popularized
by Johnny Cash's recording, Hayes, despite being a decorated hero, was
"just a Pima Indian / no water, no crops, no chance," uncomfortable
with his fame, slipping into alcoholism, and drowning in a ditch containing two inches of water. In the last verse of "Johnny Lobo," Kristofferson sees Johnny as a "phoenix rising from the ashes," referring presumably to the new directions he turned to; he met Jackson Browne and
became interested in music, specifically an interest in exploring and
illustrating the natural evolutionary process of Native oral traditions as
they continue to function for Native people. He also took up writing
poetry and acting in films. Kristofferson writes that Johnny's "warrior
heart was burnished / in the embers," and he has begun a new battle.

For some time, Kristofferson has been very supportive of Leonard
Peltier, a Native American charged with the murder of two FBI agents
in 1975; Peltier has had support from Amnesty International and numerous celebrities, who believe he was wrongly convicted of murder.
Some evidence suggests that certain testimony was coerced by the FBI.
Kristofferson has scheduled several benefit performances for Peltier,
working with Willie Nelson on one, for which the two have been
banned for life on a radio station in Southern California.

"Slouching toward the Millennium," a parody of "The Second Coming," a prophetic poem penned by Irish poet William Butler Yeats,
notes near the end of this 2000-year cycle in history that "things fall
apart; the center cannot hold," and issues a foreboding of coming evil:
"What rough beast . . . slouches toward Bethlehem to be born?" Kristofferson, concerning himself only with a thousand years, sees America as
a circus with "clowns in control," causing even the midgets to fear
"there won't be no demand for midgets anymore." The foundation of
truth and justice is disintegrating, and "it's harder to matter at all when
it's all coming down." But Kristofferson's message is, "You've still got to
do your duty to choose how you live or you die (that's just the way it is)."
In his second verse, he cites specific instances of U.S. government
intrusion, namely, the demonizing of Manuel Noriega, the bombing of
Baghdad, and the burning of the David Koresh compound at Waco,

Texas. And his final observation, "All you got to do is make them hate the victim and you're free," reinforces his warning concerning the loss of basic freedoms.

In "Sam's Song (Ask Any Working Girl)," for Sam Peckinpah, Kristofferson felt Peckinpah had been treated badly by MGM studio and proceeded to defend him against the studio's treatment. Alan Rudolph, director of *Trouble in Mind*, with Kristofferson in the lead, speaks of Kristofferson's open loyalty to Peckinpah and his public chastisement of the studio for its oppression of him. In the song, Kristofferson quotes a line from Peckinpah concerning the hardest words to be said of anyone: "They stopped you from singing your song."

In his interview on *Speaking Freely*, sponsored by the First Amendment Center in Nashville, Ken Paulson remarked to Kristofferson, "It's actually rare for somebody to publicly have an opinion now, to actually say what they believe, and write songs with conviction, and actually have their—have their life's values, their convictions, and their art all merge together" (6).

During this period, while Kristofferson continued to dwell on the loss of freedoms, basic and human, he spoke of his own struggle for personal freedom. In *Kris Kristofferson: Breakthrough*, a documentary intended as a companion piece to *Third World Warrior* and *Repossessed* yet incorporating interviews relative to his commitment to social justice, he said,

> Looking back over my life, I can see how my whole life's been a sort of a struggle for personal freedom and freedom of expression. I bailed out on several safe lives that were programmed for me by others, and in each case when I did it the feeling was exhilarating as a free fall and a little terrifying. All of it seems to have been evolving toward a freedom of expression of allowing myself to be who I was supposed to be—and I think that is what the struggle for every individual really is. (Pinkston)

7

"AIN'T YOU COME A LONG WAY DOWN THIS OLD ROAD?"

1995–2104

Despite the critical acclaim of *A Moment of Forever* (1995), Kristofferson seemed to refrain from writing more original songs and recording them. He devoted some time to new film roles, but his musical career was apparently in hiatus. In 1997, Fred Mollin, a producer making a name for himself with his project involving new recordings of the best work of songwriters, had achieved success with Jimmy Webb and was eager to follow it up with the songs of Kristofferson.

For *The Austin Sessions*, Mollin and Kristofferson agreed upon a group of songs, none of which represented his newer work, and recorded them over a period of several days at Willie Nelson's Arlyn Studios. The plan was to add the backing later, to be provided by session musicians of various backgrounds and extreme sensitivities in the interests of centering attention upon Kristofferson. Although outstanding musicians joined him on the recording, none was called upon to perform in a duet, for the purpose of the album, like Jimmy Webb's, was to allow the soon-to-be-legend to be heard singing his own songs, in his own way. Guests Jackson Browne, Vince Gill, Alison Krauss, Steve Earle, Mark Knopfler, and others contributed harmonies, while the musicians, most of whom Kristofferson had not worked with previously, aimed at a union that emphasized the ageless attributes of the songs. While new listeners were reached through these unique songs, the album's most obvious benefit was a reconnection with his fan base (Miller, 228).

Broken Freedom Song (2002) followed up *The Austin Sessions* as a compilation album of songs largely chosen from his more recent political songwriting. The album, recorded at San Francisco State University on John Prine's Oh Boy record label, began when Kristofferson was asked to contribute to a CD honoring the work of Mimi Farina, sister of Joan Baez, who had died in 2001. Once again, the musical backing, consisting of Stephen Bruton on guitar and mandolin and Keith Carper on bass, was somewhat sparse and, unlike *The Austin Sessions*, included several of his lesser-known works. Songs included some of his humorous ones, a poetic ballad, "Darby's Castle," and "Here Comes That Rainbow Again," which had been suggested to him by a scene in John Ford's film adaptation of John Steinbeck's novel *The Grapes of Wrath*. The remainder of his musical choices are "Nobody Wins," "A Moment of Forever," and "The Circle (Song for Layla Al-Attar and Los Olvidados)," a song in memory of the well-known artist killed along with her family in a 1993 U.S. bombing attack on Iraq. Reviews of the album were generally favorable, except for the inevitable complaints about his voice.

In 2006, Kristofferson, at the age of seventy, recorded *This Old Road*, his second album with producer Don Was and his first one of new material in eleven years. And while for the first album Was imported skilled session musicians from Los Angeles to provide beautifully distinctive backing for Kristofferson, this time around, Stephen Bruton on guitar, mandolin, and harmony vocals, and Kristofferson on vocals, guitar, and harmonica, along with Jim Keltner on drums and Was on acoustic bass and piano, create a minimalist, pared-down sound registering the intimacy of an ancient troubadour revealing his soul to the world. This manner of direct communication, calling for him to appear onstage, accompanied by his guitar and possibly a harmonica, and surrounded by the members of his small band, to sing songs of his own creation, had throughout his years of performing always placed him in an unbearably vulnerable situation. Yet, it was through this delivery that he had connected with his audience, confirming the shared emotions and the authenticity of his having lived the experiences of which he sang.

Now, however, the voice, smoothed to some degree, reflects the wisdom gained from seven decades of living and casts a new perspective on some of the same topics he wrote about forty years previously. In the liner notes, Don Was writes,

> This is one of the greatest records I've ever heard. The writing is so sharp, literate and wise! I keep finding new layers of nuance in each song we work on. Kris's performances are so powerful and direct!! Ephemerally, he appears to be at peace with the world and somewhat resigned to a mellower outlook. Yet, just beneath the surface, there are also layers of irony, double meaning and a fiery, rebellious spirit . . . he has poetically found a way for the two perspectives to coexist.

The simplicity of the title track features familiar images that mark the passage of time: old photographs depicting a startling and forgotten record of a life's beginnings that inspire the question "Is it really you?"; the need to remember blessings along with burdens "like the changing of the seasons"; "a face you used to know" in the looking glass presents a jarring reminder that you are "running out of time"; memories of people "you passed along the way"; and, since the overwhelming urges to hold back time proved unsuccessful, "the holy night is falling." The elegant song is so expressive of the realization that one travels down the road of the way to where he is now. The song's delivery achieves an honesty enhanced by Kristofferson's craggy voice accompanied by acoustic guitar, harmonica, mandolin, and piano.

In the songs that relate to his songwriting, "The Show Goes On" describes his experiences in the early years in Nashville with other songwriters who were all desperate for success: they would meet at night, Kristofferson remembers, and talk about rock and roll and not wanting to sell their souls; their get-togethers would frequently last all day and night in their effort "to try to sing up every soul in sight," leaving behind "anyone who couldn't see the light." This singing or creating songs with intensity, or "roaring," was the highlight of their meetings. He continues, "The sweetest thing you ever heard" was their version of legendary country music singer Roy Acuff's song "The Great Speckled Bird"; Kristofferson sings of their drinking a bucketful of booze "to try to chase away the black and the blues"; and he recollects how easy it was then at a time they could do no wrong. He recalls wistfully that "we'll never be the same again," but he understands that the show must go on. Four years after making this album, Kristofferson said to Michael Streissguth, "I wish I could sometimes go back to that time. It was just so creative. All the time. And our hearts and souls were totally committed to the songwriting" (2).

"The Last Thing to Go," in a nod to his boxing career and referring to the boxer's proverbial knees, speaks to an unidentified songwriter friend about hearing a song that sounded like one of his; immediately, he thought back to their time together when "I felt all the feelings we set down in song / torn from the body and soul." Kristofferson sings, "Love is the reason we happened at all," the love, he says, for what we were doing, which allowed us the freedom "to fall into grace." "Every true thing we wrote on the wind is still singing," and every "heartbroken rule of the road" is still alive; accompanied by acoustic guitar and harmonica, he sings, "Love is the last thing to go."

In an album that hearkens to the past for perspective on the present, "Burden of Freedom" sheds light on Kristofferson's transformation regarding the most important thing in his life. Written in 1972 and included in *Border Lord*, his second album for Fred Foster and Monument, the song reflects his fierce defense of his personal and artistic freedom and his awareness of its toll on anyone who values it. Kristofferson sings of its cost in the pain and frustration of those who love him but who do not understand his need for freedom. He pleads, "Lord, help me to shoulder the burden of freedom," and asks for help to be what he can. The song points to the loss of his family as, one by one, they are unable to live with someone who insists upon his own personal freedom at their expense. Interestingly, the song from years earlier in Kristofferson's life that called up so much pain for him and everyone who loved him is included in this album as a sign of his change in perspective. His continued quest for authenticity shows in his shift from an almost obsessive concern for his own personal or artistic freedom to an awareness that "freedom extends to everybody" (Cooper, 6). And while he had always written songs about characters on the fringes of society and was concerned with the abuse of the poor and disadvantaged, it was the concept of shared freedom and its social and political obligations and responsibilities that connected with his work for human rights. The link to his childhood near the Mexican border and his mother's fit about Anglo prejudice toward Mexicans sowed the first seeds, but the discovery of the history of the United States' manipulation and mistreatment of darker-skinned people for its own benefit was the impetus for the activism that he pursued beginning in the mid-1980s.

Many of the songs in this album revisit issues or themes from Kristofferson's life, with his drinking and carousing being one of the most widely known. "Chase the Feeling" is a reminder of the 1970s, the years when his drinking had reached epic proportions. By the end of the decade, when his second marriage had ended and he desperately wanted to maintain contact with his young daughter, he enrolled in many rehabilitation programs that required years to get clean. The speaker cites various reasons for getting loaded—hunger, problems, and demons—and repeats the line "Ain't you handsome when you're high." The speaker sarcastically insists that "nothing matters" but to "chase the feeling 'til you die." He encourages listeners to continue to indulge and "let it run your life"; and having "let it run your children off," you can easily "let it take the joy you love / and turn it to despair." The speaker invites listeners to use any excuse they choose, or just "think of number one"; nothing else matters but to "chase the feeling 'til you die."

In following the evidence of Kristofferson's evolution throughout these songs, "Pilgrim's Progress" stands out. Persons familiar with his songs recognize that the title references the title of "The Pilgrim, Chapter 33," from his 1971 album *The Silver Tongued Devil and I*. One of his more famous songs, it describes the pilgrim, whose identity was rumored to be among several different persons. But as the depiction came from Kristofferson, it more than likely refers to him. Among the various conflicting depictions given, he is said to be "a walking contradiction / partly truth and partly fiction," who is "on his lonely way back home." In "Pilgrim's Progress," Kristofferson clearly considers himself to be the pilgrim and proceeds to mark his own progress. He laments that he gets lazy and forgets his obligations, referring perhaps to those regarding his freedom or to others less fortunate. The chorus, mindful of its purpose, repeats the questions Kristofferson asks of himself concerning what he has learned over the years: "Am I strong enough to get down on my knees and pray?" And then, "Am I high enough on the chain of evolution to respect myself and my fellow humans?" Next, he declares that he should consider if he is worthy of his part in his dream that is coming true. Ironically, the doubts that plague him about his worthiness plagued him similarly back in 1972 and appeared in the enormously popular song, "Why Me," that grew possibly out of his guilt about having disappointed his family. The self-appraisal in "Pilgrim's Progress" suggests he may have had some doubts of being worthy of his success, his renown, and his friends and family—in fact, the happiness he seems to have achieved.

In "In the News," Kristofferson laments the state of affairs in America, by way of the news coverage in the early 2000s. The first and last verses address the murder of Laci Peterson by her husband, who "chained her to a heavy thing and threw her in the water"; the verses form bookends for other notorious news stories that dominated the spotlight. And while he calls up global warming, and the vast amount of money required to bomb a "nation on its knees," his fervid political consciousness takes on the United States' "Holy War" on Iraq and the blasphemy of tying divine will to human agendas. "Anyone not marching to their tune they call it treason," Kristofferson sings. "Everyone says God is on his side." But he goes on to indicate that he had heard God say, "Not in my name, not on my ground." But for the suffering, he sings, "Don't blame God. I swear . . . he's crying too." He emphasizes the human tragedy by dwelling on the "broken dreamers, broken rules / broken-hearted people," and logs a protest against not only the events that occurred during the George W. Bush administration, but the values of that administration as well.

An answer to the disregard for human life displayed by the United States in its invasion of Iraq, excoriated in "In the News," is to be found in "Holy Creation," Kristofferson's song about the sanctity of children. The song's title itself suggests a reference to William Blake's assertion that "everything that lives is holy," while the song describes a child, presumably one of his own children, holding his mother, "with his head on her shoulder," singing love songs to her.

"Thank You for a Life," a tribute to Lisa, his wife of twenty-three years (in 2006) and the mother of their five children, is also a tribute to her influence upon him: "Everything I am I owe to you," he sings. His gratitude for their children is followed by his gratitude for "the sadness that you saved me from the madness," he sings, using the familiar wordplay for which he is famous. He makes note of the lift in his outlook because of his life with her. The song offers a perspective on Kristofferson's life that seems fitting for an album appearing in his seventieth year.

The tenth song in this album, "Final Attraction," was composed twenty years earlier, as Kristofferson remembered a time when he, waiting in the wings, observed Willie Nelson on stage closing a show. Kristofferson speaks of Nelson's final attraction as his "finest performance / approaching perfection" and likens it to "some kind of love." "Somewhere in your lifetime," he sings of himself and others: "You were dared into feeling" and were torn apart by many emotions. He goes on to say the audience loves you for sharing their sorrows, "so pick up that guitar / go break a heart." At the beginning of the song, "To Beat the Devil" (1970), he listed his struggling friends, reaching for peace and love; at the end of "Final Attraction," in 2006, he closes with a list of masterful performers who have already moved down this old road and, now gone, have reached a new dimension of their art and their place in the culture. For Hank Williams, Janis Joplin, Waylon Jennings, John Lennon, Roger Miller, Jimi Hendrix, Mickey Newbury, and "maybe one time for me / go break a heart."

In 2009, Kristofferson recorded *Closer to the Bone*, showing what life is like from this end of the road. Originally titled *Starlight and Stone*, he changed the title to *Closer to the Bone*, also produced at New West Studios, insisting that closer to the bone means nearer to the truth. Also produced by Don Was, this album is a stark performance that, from the standpoint of renewal or reaffirmation of performance ability, has been seen to offer much the same opportunity for Kristofferson as Rick Rubin did for Johnny Cash in his later years. When approached with that question, Kristofferson backed away from the idea, saying, "Don Was was the guy who really suggested that I be recording like this" (Schneider).

"Emotionally, 'Closer to the Bone' is very much like 'This Old Road,'" says Kristofferson, who goes on to say,

> Every album I've made has been about making sense of my life at the time. *Closer to the Bone* is a reflective album. It's about making sense of life at this end of the game. I used to do records about a year apart with music covering issues of human rights, military aggression or whatever was going on in the world. These last two records have been more reflective about my own life. (Graff, 1)

Of the approach to the method of production, Was notes that for *This Old Road*, he had attempted to create the experience of Kristofferson sitting three feet away from his audience as he sang ten songs. "People really seemed to respond positively to that," says Was, "so we went for the same effect on this new album . . . to eliminate everything that creates distance between the listener and Kris" (Graff, 1).

In an album filled with intimate songs and marked with simple melodies, Kristofferson's voice brings forth the words unimpeded by forceful production. Besides his vocals, acoustic guitar, and harmonica, and Stephen Bruton's harmony vocals, guitar, and mandolin, the veteran drummer Jim Keltner, and Was on piano and percussion form a spare backing ensemble that underscores the earnestness of the lyrics. The title track sets the tone for the entire album as the speaker proclaims "everything is sweeter/closer to the bone" and confirms that the songs come from his heartbeat and speak of "nothing but the truth now." The speaker celebrates getting older and better and making pretty music that is closer to one's feelings but finds it "kinda funny" that this happens when you're "running out of time." He says he's "not afraid of moonlight"; he has no fear, as he is "soaring like an eagle" and "skipping like a stone" as he sails "over the horizon." He emphasizes he is "open to the pleasure" and "equal to the pain." The backing on this song is notably performed by Bruton and his beautifully expressive harmony vocal and mandolin. He passed away at age sixty following the completion of the sessions, and the album is a memorial to him. "I can't think of Stephen without heartbreak," says Kristofferson, remembering this experiences with Bruton, who first came to work with him at the age of twenty. "We were soul brothers. I'm just grateful that he was able to play on this" (Graff, 2).

The second selection, "From Here to Forever," written by Kristofferson for his children and accompanied by Rami Jaffe on the piano, was so perfectly rendered by Jaffe that it made Kristofferson weep. He said, "I can understand Stephen being in sync with me, but I'd never met Rami before" (Flippo, "Conversation"). As his child sleeps, he urges him to fill his heart with love for his long journey, where his guide will be the love that will "live like a song in [his] soul." The bridge then proposes that if a time should come when "we're not together," he should remember his words: "I'll be there wherever you go." From his own hard-won wisdom, Kristofferson points out that there are many ways to stumble, and "someday your heart's going to break." He advises him against being hasty, imploring him to "be all you know you can be," and then, in a tender, fatherly manner, says that if he needs a reason for living, to "do it for love and for me." Kristofferson says in this song that the vision of one of his children smiling in his sleep was the "answer to anyone's prayer," and this song is every parent's prayer for his children.

"Holy Woman," a love song to his wife Lisa, and to womankind in general, is one of the instances of Kristofferson's skill with working on more than one level. He has said,

> To me, the best love songs work on two—maybe three—different levels where you're talking about the person who you're right opposite and all the people like that. I feel like sometimes when I'm singing a song like "Moment of Forever" that it goes both to your significant other and to the audience. . . . I think the best love songs I've written work on that level, like "Help Me Make It through the Night" is as much to the audience as it is to whoever you were singing about in the first place. (Flippo, "Conversation")

He depicts the holy woman three times, all exhibiting her exceptionality: First, he sings, "I see you in the morning with your spirit to the sky," with freedom in the air, coming like an angel "to show me how to fly" beyond the mess of manmade affairs. Second, he sings, "I see you in the darkness with the moonlight on your face," and feels their faces coming together into space. The third depiction of the holy woman is at night "in the glory of your passion burning bright" when "you held me in the darkness." In the chorus, Kristofferson proclaims that he will build a monument to her and, declaring he is only human, ends with the line "Can you fill the holy emptiness / in me."

"Starlight and Stone" is a strange waltz, with words spoken by a warrior who has kept a promise that was hard to keep. While he says he is "heading for home," he ruminates on his own steadfastness, and despite the deep silence and long nights, he pledges that "I'm still your man." The situation seems to have provoked a great deal of stress for both the speaker and his mate, as the look on her face that "the world can't erase" provokes his belief that "the soul never dies."

Of the three tributes in the album, the first one, "Sister Sinead," for Sinead O'Connor, the Irish singer who garnered almost universal condemnation when she, at a guest appearance on *Saturday Night Live* in

1992, ripped apart a photo of Pope John Paul II in a protest against child abuse in the Catholic Church. Two weeks later, at the Bob Dylan thirtieth anniversary tribute in Madison Square Garden, she was met by loud audience jeers and promptly ran into Kristofferson's arms, whereupon he could be heard on the mic saying to her, "Don't let the bastards get you down." That Kristofferson admires O'Connor for speaking up for what she believes despite the widespread denunciation of her should go without saying, in view of his persistent activism against the U.S. government for foreign policies he found repugnant. In the song he sings for her, "concerning the God-awful mess that she made"; he says when she told "her truth" to the world, it "profoundly was misunderstood." He sings of the condemnation from around the world that was heaped upon "that bald-headed brave little girl." He acknowledges she asked for trouble because of her prominent target, but he observes that while some candles flicker and fade, some "burn as true as my sister Sinead." In the chorus, he sings, "And maybe she's crazy and maybe she ain't" and, offering an unusual appraisal of art and piety, adds, "But so is Picasso and so are the saints."

The next song in *Closer to the Bone* is "Hall of Angels," a song "dedicated to Eddie Rabbitt's lost child." Much like the preceding song about Sinead O'Connor's ordeal, this song is concerned with a severe challenge in the life of singer Eddie Rabbitt. His son, Timmy, was born with a debilitating disease that required a liver transplant, and he remained on life support for two years before a donor was finally found. But after the surgery, Timmy's body rejected the new liver, and Timmy lapsed into a coma and died. Kristofferson sings of drinking at a bar with a friend to the memory of a "lady who loved him and died," and they could find no reason to go on. Suddenly, a stranger came in from the dark and "turned us around with a song." The stranger sang of his daughter who had died; his grief was so overpowering he wanted to die also. But he had a "dream or a vision" that caused him to see things differently. In his dream, he saw a group of shining young angels, each one holding a "bright, burning candle," but not his angel. When he asked why her candle was not burning like the others, she said, "Oh, Daddy, each time that I try to light it / your tears just keep drowning the flame." Kristofferson's song ends with feelings of awe for the stranger whose "spirit was truly alive" and with his realization that everyone who has ever loved him will live in the "hall of the angels," as long as the love is in his heart.

The seventh song, "Love Don't Live Here Anymore," first appeared in *Natural Act* (1978), Kristofferson's and Coolidge's last duo album together, and seems to indicate their marriage was all but over. They divorced in 1979, ushering in a period of pain and anger for him that was very challenging on both personal and professional levels. He did not want the divorce and was surprised by it. "It was as devastating as anything I've ever been through," he says. "I thought the marriage would last forever" (McCall, 3). Coolidge was heartbroken by his habits while on the road and could endure them no longer. The end to his marriage was only part of that difficult time period in his life. His solo recording career was dwindling while Coolidge's was in the ascendant; whereas early in their marriage he was clearly the dominant force, by 1979 she was at her peak—her records were outselling his, and their venues were largely more impressive because of her. Plus, they had contractual obligations to fulfill and were forced to sing together on television and at various functions during the time before the impending divorce. During some of this time, Kristofferson was in Montana filming *Heaven's Gate*, directed by Michael Cimino, who spoke later of the "black Lincolnesque moods" that Kristofferson would sink into because of his despair concerning the divorce. Uppermost in Kristofferson's mind at that time was his five-year-old daughter Casey, whom he feared would be lost to him much like his older children. Unwilling to attempt to cheer him up, Cimino has said that since the film's story was a dark one, he worked Kristofferson's black mood into his character and role in the film (*Kris Kristofferson: His Life and Work*). However, the film itself also became a part of his misery, as it turned out to be a gigantic bomb. Also, clearly associated with the distress of this time was his continuing battle with alcohol; he had famously stopped drinking back in 1976 after watching *A Star Is Born* and imagining his family's anguish should the fate of his character befall him. However, he still had issues with drinking and was in and out of various rehab centers in California. But as Kristofferson continues to affirm, "The beauty of dropping to the bottom is that it wipes the slate clean" (McCall, 3).

"Love Don't Live Here Anymore" contains images that express the idea that nothing of the couple's relationship or life together remains: they behave toward each other as total strangers; photographs and relics are scattered on the floor to ensure that nothing binds them to each other or to the years of their union; they share nothing; they don't care; and he has nothing to say that would interest her. He says, "There's no happy ending," and the song ends with, "Love don't live here anymore." This song, like several in this album, depicts an excruciating episode in his life. Jeff Giddens, reviewer from *No Depression*, says of *Closer to the Bone* that it is not for the "faint of heart" because it looks squarely at some very difficult situations. The album, says Giddens, "contains no songs about country people, barroom bad decisions, or about automobiles of any kind. Instead, Kris doesn't waste a second in relating that life is as much about the hard challenges you face . . . as much as it is about the people you are surrounded with" (2). Vowing to tell the truth in the album, Kristofferson kept his word as each song confronts a significant, meaningful event in his life.

"Good Morning John" is a song to his idol, Johnny Cash, on the occasion of his returning home from rehab. Kristofferson was asked by Cash's wife, June Carter Cash, to write a song to welcome Cash home and perform it at a celebratory sobriety dinner for him and a few close friends and family. The song, although somewhat embarrassing for both Cash and Kristofferson, was a gesture of the love and concern his family had for him. Fairly lengthy, it says good morning to him and his future; it relates everyone's worry; and it reminds him of the inspiration he has become. Kristofferson sings words of encouragement to Cash, mostly to "keep smiling, John," because he owes that to others and to himself, the "dark and holy wonder that you are." Kristofferson continues his encouragement to Cash, saying that on the rocky road to glory, it is the "straightest and the strongest" that will survive. He congratulates Cash for all his accomplishments, and at the end, he reminds Cash that while he might lose his mind or his memory, you "ain't gonna lose me / as your friend." As it turned out, this visit to the Betty Ford Center was Cash's last visit to rehab, but as Jonathan Silverman, author of the thought-provoking *Nine Choices: Johnny Cash and American Culture* maintains, "He probably did not really kick the drugs until he died" (32). The song was supposed to have been recorded by the Highwaymen, but as Kristofferson relays, "When I got to the line that said 'I love you,' Willie Nelson said, 'He loves you John' and we all cracked up laughing. We never finished it, so I finished it myself" (Graff, 2). One of the more confessional songs in the album, "Tell Me One More Time," is an open admission of a deep, profound love. Sung as an old-time gospel song, and accompanied only by Kristofferson's acoustic guitar and his harmonica, it communicates in a most intimate manner "what is on his heart." He feels forgiven and is now interested in living after coming very close to "giving up the ghost." Speaking plainly about what he has to offer, he admits he won't be surprised if she leaves, and he will go on living. But he asks her, before she makes her decision, to tell him one more time: "Did you feel a little lightning / did you feel a little thunder" that was just barely under control? Was it startling to stare into the "deep and starry splendor of your soul?"

Closer to the Bone wields powerful memories from past experiences. In "Let the Walls Come Down," the speaker remembers an "old soul" standing on a dark corner singing "his heart right out at a world / passing him by." He also remembers every word of the song nobody heard as he cried out, "Let the walls come down." The speaker continues with a plea to let love show through and "help your brother in need," and ends with the perception that "you can't free nobody else / if you can't be true to yourself." The song begins with the voice of Kristofferson and his acoustic guitar and gently swells to include Keltner's drums, Bruton's mandolin, and the harmony on the chorus vocals. The remembered words of the "old soul" on the corner and others like him have been catalysts in Kristofferson's own metamorphosis.

The meditative spirit of the album may be best seen in the last song, "The Wonder," in which Kristofferson swears "to be thankful for the rest of my days" and also to be worthy of the chance he has had "to live and believe / in the love and the wonder of you." Before he found Lisa, his wife, he felt sad at the end of the day as the light slipped away; the heavens were empty like dreams that never would come true until love blessed the skies and his heart "with the wonder of you." The simple melody and beautiful words emanating from Kristofferson's gruff voice, accompanied only by his acoustic guitar and harmonica, take on an ethereal air, whereby the events are moved into a realm beyond mundane affairs. The entire album, however, benefits greatly from the toned-down backing music that allows the songs and their messages to come through clearly.

During breaks in his touring schedule, Kristofferson found time to write more songs and recorded *Feeling Mortal*, released in January 2013, the first on his own KK record label almost four years after *Closer to the Bone*; sessions were completed in three days, with twenty tracks in all, and ten chosen for the album. Also produced by Don Was, the album features pared-down musical accompaniment, with a clear interest in making the most of Kristofferson's vocals. The stellar studio musicians at work in the album—guitarist Mark Goldenberg, pedal steel master Greg Leiz, keyboardist Matt Rollins, violinist and vocalist Sara Watkins, bassist Sean Hurley, and drummer Aaron Sterling—provide restrained backing that allows Kristofferson's raw, emotional lyrics center stage as they set forth his hard look at life and his unflinching stare into the face of death.

The title track begins with his familiar rough-hewn voice proclaiming, "Wide awake and feeling mortal," and proceeds to investigate what he feels at this point in his life. "Here today and gone tomorrow / that's the way it's gotta be" is a soul-baring, matter-of-fact observation confronting the inevitable fate of all human beings. Don Was says not to believe that Kristofferson is preparing to leave the world. He continues,

> I think all great artists write to their points of view at any given moment. I don't think this should be viewed as the final word from Kris Kristofferson, despite the grim title. But it's very interesting to get the global perspective of a 76-year-old who's really lived in this world and who has squeezed a lot of living into those 76 years. It's interesting to see where he's at now and how his perspective on what's important has changed over the years. I think the album really is a primer in remaining fiercely independent, yet finding a state of acceptance and gratitude and grace regarding the way things are. (Lewis, "Feeling Mortal," 2)

"God Almighty! Here I am," Kristofferson sings. "Is it where I ought to be?" Amazed he is still alive, he realizes he will soon be descending "like the sun into the sea." He looks in the mirror and sees an old man with a "shaky self-esteem"; questioned about his "shaky self-esteem" by a surprised interviewer, Kristofferson responds, "It's been a part of me all of my life" (Margolis, 2). But, he admits, he is not too concerned with that now, his primary interest being his gratitude for just being here. He gives thanks to God "for the artist that You are" and also for "the man You made of me."

The second song on the album, "Mama Stewart," refers to the ninety-four-year-old grandmother of Rita Coolidge, Kristofferson's second ex-wife, who reportedly kept a family album and wrote songs about all the grandchildren. In the song, Mama Stewart is blind and because of her years has become forthright in her speech, and she surprises Kristofferson by saying "things that I'd grown too blind to see." His visit with her awakened "feelings that I'd hidden deep inside," and he was "thankful she couldn't see / the sudden tears I couldn't hide." Although she had, at the age of seven, travelled west in a wagon train, she took a plane to California for eye surgery, reporting in her trip that "she'd got too close to heaven" and felt she might be going all the way. When her vision was restored, she "didn't even seem at all surprised." In the chorus, he sings, "Everything is beautiful in Mama Stewart's eyes" and ends with "Lord, let me see what Mama Stewart sees."

Kristofferson's continued emphasis on things of importance at this time in his life calls forth a rip-roaring reinforcement of the necessity of music. "Bread for the Body" tells of his jettisoning of materialistic icons such as houses and cars in recognition of his need for a simpler life of physical and spiritual nourishment. He says, "I'm living my life by the lesson I've learned," paying no mind to the bridges that have been burned; the time, he believes, that comprises one's life "was meant to be spent and not meant to be saved." He does not care if some people think him a fool, because "life is a song for the dying to sing," and it means nothing without feeling. He believes an individual can exist "without silver or gold" if he has "bread for the body and song for the soul."

"You Don't Tell Me What to Do" appears to provide an answer to all those who think he should not continue touring and making appearances across the country and outside the United States into Europe, Asia, Australia, New Zealand, and Africa. He says he belongs on the highway "losing myself in the soul of a song," as well as "losing myself in the fight for the right to be righteously wrong." Kristofferson begins singing in a soft voice that becomes more matter of fact as it goes along, and probably leaves no listeners with any desire to change his mind, or any doubt that he has followed this pattern his whole life. As a totally independent person, he goes on to say that he sings his own songs, he drinks when he's thirsty, and he will make music, whiskey, and love as long as the spirit inside me "says you don't tell me what to do." Since he has left his future behind he sees no reason to change his mind, and anyone who tries to is wasting his time. "The message in that song," says

Kristofferson, "has been a real part of my life, because I've certainly gone my own way and spoken my own words" (Hughes, 1).

"Stairway to the Bottom" appears to be yet another cheating song in a genre that thrives on them. To Lynne Margolis, Kristofferson identifies this song as an early one he wrote in Nashville that was "sort of autobiographical." He conceded, "I was pretty critical of myself and others at that time" (2). The speaker speaks in the first verse to someone cheating with the wife of a friend and hoping he could forget it; the speaker tells the cheater the wine he is drinking will not keep him from thinking "of the bitter taste that lingers in your soul." The speaker moves along reminding the cheating man of his lies and the fact that the person he cheats with means nothing to him; the speaker watches the man in the mirror on the wall and understands he takes pride in deceiving one who once believed in him and knows that the lies and each broken vow create a "new nail in the coffin of your soul." The song has become a strong statement about shame, reproach, and having to live with oneself. No one, the speaker says, is crying for your love as you betray a trust. "Look around you on that stairway to the bottom," he says. "No one's watching but that mirror on the wall."

"Just Suppose" pictures a "what if" situation that seems to depict the true situation. The speaker, who turns out to be part of the triangle, asks the wayward husband if he supposes his wife will still be crying when he returns, similar to all the other times, and if he imagines he'll say he's sorry, as he had always done; since he had been away for some time, would he blame her if she had been untrue? At that point, the speaker, asks the husband if he expects him to feel guilty "for not giving back the love you threw away"; in the final twist, the speaker/lover asks the husband to suppose that if he really loved her now, "what do you suppose you'd do if you were me?"

"Castaway" details a strange experience. Once while sailing the Caribbean, the speaker saw a small abandoned fishing vessel drifting aimlessly; with its tattered sails and damaged wheel, he thought "the little boat sure looks a lot like me." He pulled alongside, boarded, and explored the empty area below, realizing even more completely that the "vessel was the sister of my soul." His footsteps seemed like echoes in a cave that "seemed to say there ain't no way to leave this floating grave"; and when he got back to the deck, his "ship had vanished like a dream." Because a rudderless ship just drifts, "each day I'm drawing closer to the brink"; he envisions himself as "just a speck upon the waters" of an immense ocean. He says, "I won't even make a ripple when I sink."

Kristofferson's song coauthored with Shel Silverstein, "My Heart Was the Last One to Know," is an older song written in the 1960s and recorded by country music artist Connie Smith in 1967. About the writing of the song, Kristofferson said, "I was just writing about heart-break that I was going through and doing it the way the people I admired like Hank Williams would've handled it." (Atkinson). Reminiscent of his earlier songs, this one achieves much of its impact from its internal rhyme and devices that promote near rhyme or call attention to certain repeated sounds. The phrasing is quite smooth.

The final song in *Feeling Mortal* is "Ramblin' Jack," a tribute to Kristofferson's hard-living friend, Ramblin' Jack Elliott. The son of a Brooklyn doctor, Elliott Charles Adnopoz rebelled against his parents' expectations that he become a doctor and instead ran away to join the rodeo. Jack came onto the music landscape in the 1950s and has been active since then. Influenced by Woody Guthrie, he in turn influenced Bob Dylan and various singers on to the Rolling Stones and the Grateful Dead. Ramblin' Jack has "got a face like a tumbled down shack," says Kristofferson, and he's been "known to lay his weary head / in some funky, unfamiliar beds." In the chorus, Kristofferson sings that he knows Ramblin' Jack "ain't afraid of where he's going," and he feels sure "he ain't ashamed of where he's been"; every seed he has sowed has been paid for with a bit of his soul, "and he made his own mistakes, and love, and friends / ain't that what matters in the end." Was insists Kristofferson's assessment of Elliott is universal commentary. "It's about all of us, really. . . . That's everybody" (Lewis, "Feeling Mortal," 3). The song was written by Kristofferson in two parts—the first part years ago and the last part more recently. Ramblin' Jack, who was eighty-two at the time of this album's release, is remembered for his smile and the "laughter in his eyes"; and since Ramblin' Jack's life was music, Kristofferson believes he would be truly surprised if he knew how well he had sung every song. He insists Ramblin' Jack must have a lucky star while out on the road "mixing up the music in his soul." This tribute came from Kristofferson's admiration of Jack "just for being the one-dimensional person he is," says Kristofferson, laughing. "He's never changed a bit and he never will" (Lewis, "Feeling Mortal," 3).

The songs in this album, similar to his early songs, reflect his feelings when they were written. Chiefly about old age and death, the songs bring from him a wry comment: "I'm definitely feeling mortal, and just about all of them have an autobiographical element. It's that end of the race and you can't help but think about it. But I've got so many things to be grateful for. This is the best part of my life" (Hughes, 1–2).

8

CONCLUSION

Kris Kristofferson's odyssey through the world of country music is unique and unprecedented. That he who was not easily categorized chose Nashville, whose music establishment had followed unwritten rules and traditions for generations, as the place that would allow him to express his repressed emotion is an inescapable irony. Despite the Nashville sound's push into the softer violins and background vocals, aiming to lure pop music listeners, the pure country music that Kristofferson favored was regimented in form, style, and subject matter. But the customary focus on the plaintive voice directly expressing raw emotion, first and always associated with Hank Williams, held, for the alienated son of a military family, his only hope for self-expression.

After five years of day-to-day struggling, Kristofferson emerged as a prolific songwriter whose songs immediately captivated the musical public and had it clamoring for more. But it had not been easy. His parents disowned him because he had abandoned a promising military career; his transition to Nashville with its subsequent poverty and shady lifestyles of songwriters cost him his marriage; his creative-writing college degree and Rhodes scholar education at Oxford became handicaps that required overcompensation to produce the correct country vernacular; his innate liberal viewpoint toward the poor, disadvantaged, and society's outcasts was not particularly supported by Music Row; and his own voice was so disagreeably gravelly that he was not even allowed to record his own songs, but instead provided great recording opportunities for numerous top artists with melodious voices.

When Fred Foster, the second producer to be convinced of Kristof-ferson's talent—the first being Marijohn Wilkin—offered him a ten-year solo recording contract that required original material, the pros-pects of finally being in a position to express himself were staggering. The songs that had awaited expression for years were filled with a direct openness that was perceived by the music establishment as a violation of its values. Kristofferson became the leader in a group of young song-writers known as the "new breed," who were credited with bringing change to country music. Bill Malone, country music historian, says, "Sometimes self-consciously poetic, the new writers were probably more important for what they said, rather than for how they said it: they opened up new realms of expression for country singers and writers" (Malone and Neal, 306). The honesty about relationships that Kristof-ferson felt a need to express required a different language than the "little rhyming songs" (*Kris Kristofferson: His Life and Work*) that in his mind made up popular music; and despite country music's vague and clichéd wording, he valued the reality of its subject matter. But his own intimate phrasing drew the criticism of Music Row producers, as well as some television producers and DJs who would not play the recordings on the radio.

Other songs written by Kristofferson that were quite popular were the longer ballad songs concerning characters, many of whom were on the edge of society or were victims of injustice, and some songs that acerbically depicted middle-class values. The merging of his own pain and loneliness with the countercultural values of the 1960s resulted in an alienation from everything middle class or authoritarian—as demon-strated in many of his early songs whose lines contain forbidden words relating to drug use or the word "blacks," referring to African Americans. Eventually, so many of Kristofferson's classic songs had been recorded by himself as well as a number of the most prominent, significant recording artists in the industry, and had endeared them-selves to a huge number of Kristofferson followers, that the artists and fans insisted upon the directness and honesty of the lyrics.

Of Kristofferson's hundreds of songs, he will most likely be remem-bered for his early songs, written at first blush of a career that took the musical world of the 1970s by storm. "Me and Bobby McGee," his countercultural anthem concerning freedom and its burden; "Sunday Morning Coming Down," a description of his hangover that suggests an alcoholic's losses are a burden of freedom; "For the Good Times," the painful end of a relationship; "Help Me Make It through the Night," a depiction of the devastation of loneliness; "Loving Her Was Easier," the memory of a perfect love that ended; "To Beat the Devil," recounting his confrontation with the devil who tempted him to give up during a particularly difficult period in his early songwriting struggles; "The Silver Tongued Devil and I," displaying the devil working as a facilitator for womanizing; and "The Pilgrim, Chapter 33," a self-defining song, employing the famous line "a walking contradiction" are prime examples of the scope of his creativity. Kristofferson's lyrics are direct, honest, and confessional, and his emotional songs connect with his audience in a passionate recognition of his authenticity. Several other songs in his first few albums spoke to the social unrest of the time period and, at the same time, set standards that many other songwriters sought in vain to achieve.

Besides his extensive self-expression as a classic songwriter and film actor, his activism during the 1980s brought about widespread criticism, especially from the more conservative members in society, including the country music sector, and wreaked havoc with his recording career. As a son of a military family who had served three tours of duty in Germany, he suffered extreme disillusionment from learning the extent of the U.S. government's deception about its real intentions in Vietnam. Sensing a repeat of that pretense in Central America, he saw it as his moral obligation to write songs of protest. His two albums, *Repossessed* (1986) and *Third World Warrior* (1990), ran the gamut from laments for martyred heroes to songs of dismay for America's loss of integrity, praise for Nicaraguan warriors and heroes, anguish over innocent victims, and a song for Vietnam veterans, "Shipwrecked in the 80s," an anthem for the government's abandonment of its heroes.

During a particularly frazzled time in Chicago, when he was ragged and ill from overwork, walking pneumonia, and alcoholism, Kristofferson was able to catch the act of Steve Goodman, who opened for him, and his friend John Prine, also from Chicago and performing at another club. Stunned, Kristofferson listened to Prine as he sang every song he had written and arranged for both Goodman and Prine to accompany him to the Bitter End in New York for guest spots. He also enlisted Canadian songwriter and entertainer Paul Anka to help secure recording contracts for both. Ironically, Prine idolized Kristofferson much the same way as Kristofferson revered Johnny Cash. Known to be extremely generous with his friends, Kristofferson helped some out with bills they owed, he financed the production and recording of *Old Five and Dimers Like Me* for his friend Billy Joe Shaver, and was always ready to contribute in any way possible to benefit performances for friends or causes.

Kristofferson lore about his beginnings in Nashville spread far and wide, convincing many young, ambitious, talented singer-songwriters that if Kristofferson could go there and with hard work, dedication, and the camaraderie of other like-minded songwriters make it to the top, then they could too. Two of the more talented Kristofferson imitators were Guy Clark and Rodney Crowell, both from Texas, who came to Nashville to become songwriters. Clark, who arrived in 1971, says, "He was my milepost. He wrote in a way that no one had ever heard before. Or you thought you'd heard it, but it was the first time you heard it. Kris has a real respect for the language, a student of poetry and a poet himself" (Streissguth, 85). Crowell, from a poor family, came to Nashville in 1972, prepared to live or die by his passion for music. In his tribute to Kristofferson for winning the Lifetime Achievement Award at the Grammy Awards in January 2014, Crowell said,

> By creating a narrative style that introduced intelligence, humor, emotional eloquence, spiritual longing, male vulnerability, and a devilish sensuality—indeed a form of eroticism—to country music, Kris Kristofferson, without compromising the content and quality of his work, did as much to expose the mainstream accessibility of an all-too-often misunderstood art form as Roy Acuff, Hank Williams, Johnny Cash, Roger Miller, Willie Nelson, Ray Charles (I'm thinking Modern Sounds in Country & Western Music) and, more recently, Garth Brooks. (Crowell)

During a five-minute break in Kristofferson's concert in Cape Town, South Africa, in March 2014, *Rolling Stone*'s William Welfare talked with Kristofferson, age seventy-seven, who said, "I make no claim for my singing or musicianship, but I am a good songwriter" (Kristofferson, Welfare interview). Indeed. His songs that he continues to sing to enthusiastic and grateful audiences in packed auditoriums both in the United States and abroad, and have been recorded by around five hundred artists, are essentially timeless. They are not just country songs;

they have been beautifully performed by pop, jazz, and blues artists, as the feelings they display are universal. But as evidenced by the number of people who still attend his shows, he can still connect emotionally with his audience and can communicate his songs better than anyone. Forty-four years ago, when Kristofferson was offered a ten-year song-writing/recording contract by Fred Foster, he said, "Man, I can't sing. I sound like a frog." And Foster's rejoinder, "Yes, but a frog that can communicate," still rings in the air (Streissguth, 56).

FURTHER READING

Atkinson, Brian T. "Kris Kristofferson Lives and Writes without Regret." *CMT Edge*, January 14, 2013. http://www.cmtedge.com/.

Balchunas, Michael. "Acts of Will." *Pomona College Magazine Online* 41, no. 2 (winter 2004): 1–4. http://www.pomona.edu/.

Bane, Michael. *The Outlaws: Revolution in Country Music.* N.p.: Country Music Magazine Press, 1978.

———. *Willie: An Unauthorized Biography of Willie Nelson.* New York: Dell, 1984.

Blake, William. *The Complete Writings of William Blake.* Edited by Geoffrey Keynes. Oxford: Oxford University Press, 1966.

Bowman, David. "Kris Kristofferson." *Salon.* September 24, 1999. http://www.salon.com/.

Bufwack, Mary A., and Robert K. Oermann. *Finding Her Voice: Women in Country Music 1800–2000.* Nashville: Country Music Foundation Press, Vanderbilt University Press, 2003.

Burke, Tom. "Kris Kristofferson Sings the Good-Life Blues." *Esquire*, December 1976, 126–28, 206, 210.

———. "Kristofferson's Talking Blues." *Country Music Review*, October 1974, part 1, 23–26.

———. "Kristofferson's Talking Blues." *Country Music Review*, November 1974, part 2, 20–22.

Campbell, Joseph. *The Power of Myth, with Bill Moyers.* New York: Doubleday, 1988.

Cantwell, David. *Merle Haggard: The Running Kind (American Music Series).* Austin: University of Texas Press, 2013.

Cantwell, David, and Bill Friskics-Warren. *Heartaches by the Number: Country Music's 500 Greatest Singles.* Nashville: Country Music Foundation Press, Vanderbilt University Press, 2003.

Carrier, Scott. "What I've Learned: Kris Kristofferson." *Esquire*, May 1, 1999, 2.

Cartwright, Gary. "A Star Is Reborn." *Texas Monthly*, March 1997. http://www.texasmonthly.com/.

Cash, Johnny. "Kris Kristofferson (1936–): Actor, Songwriter, Singer." Taken from the booklet for *The Winning Hand.* Murat Shriners Organization. Accessed December 17, 2014. http://www.muratshrine.org/.

Cash, Johnny, with Patrick Carr. *Johnny Cash: The Autobiography.* New York: Harper, 1997.

Clark, Guy. Interviewed by Dan McIntosh. *Songwriter Interviews* (blog). Songfacts, August 5, 2011. http://www.songfacts.com/.

Comtois, Kevin. *Troubadours and Troublemakers: The Evolution of American Protest Music.* Charleston, SC: CreateSpace Independent Publishing Platform, 2013. Kindle edition.

Cooper, Peter. "Freedom's Still the Most Important Thing for Me: A Conversation with Kris Kristofferson." *No Depression* 53, January–February 2005. http://archives.nodepression. com/.

———. "Kris Kristofferson Reflects on Life, Death and Friendship." *Music* (blog). *Tennessean*, October 2, 2009. http://blogs.tennessean.com/.

Crowe, Cameron. "Rita Coolidge Biography." *Uncool*, 1978. Accessed December 17, 2014. http://www.theuncool.com/.

Crowell, Rodney. "Lifetime Achievement Award: Kris Kristofferson." Grammy.com, January 22, 2014. http://www.grammy.com/.

Dawidoff, Nicholas. *In the Country of Country: A Journey to the Roots of American Music.* New York: Random House Vintage, 2011.

Deusner, Stephen. "Hillbillies, Outlaws, and Songwriting Legends: The Legacy of Nashville's Ryman Auditorium." *American Songwriter*, July 22, 2014. http://www. americansongwriter.com/.

Dunkerley, Beville. "Willie Nelson, Sheryl Crow 'Walk the Line' to Salute Johnny Cash." *Boot*, August 2, 2012. http://theboot.com/.

Dylan, Bob. *Chronicles.* Vol. 1. New York: Simon & Schuster, 2004.

Eals, Clay. *Steve Goodman: Facing the Music.* Toronto: ECW Press, 2007.

Earle, Steve. "Kris Kristofferson Story: Rita on Their Divorce." BBC, November 2008. https://www.youtube.com/.

Escott, Colin. *Hank Williams: The Biography.* New York: Little, Brown, 1994.

———. *Lost Highway: The True Story of Country Music.* Washington, DC: Smithsonian Books, 2003.

Flippo, Chet. "A Conversation with Kris Kristofferson." Nashville Skyline. *CMT News*, October 1, 2009. http://www.cmt.com/news.

———. "Country Music: The Rock and Roll Influence." *Rolling Stone*, December 20, 1973, 15–16.

———. "Outlaws All Over Again." Nashville Skyline. *CMT News*, May 20, 2013. http://www. cmt.com/news.

Friskics-Warren, Bill. "Kris Kristofferson: 'To Beat the Devil'; Intimations of Immortality." *No Depression* 62, March–April 2006. http://archives.nodepression.com/.

Giddens, Jeff. "Album Review: Kris Kristofferson—*Closer to the Bone*." *No Depression*, September 22, 2009. http://nodepression.com/.

Graff, Gary. "Kris Kristofferson Latest Cuts: *Closer to the Bone*." *Billboard*, July 27, 2009. http://www.billboard.com/.

Grantham, Dewey W. *The South in Modern America: A Region at Odds.* New American Nation Series. Fayetteville: University of Arkansas Press, 2001.

Greene, Andy. "Flashback: Sinead O'Connor Booed Offstage at Bob Dylan Celebration." *Rolling Stone*, November 19, 2013. http://www.rollingstone.com/.

Hamilton, Neil Alexander. *Outlaws Still at Large: A Saga of Roots Country.* Charleston, SC: CreateSpace Independent Publishing Platform, 2013. Kindle edition.

Heath, Chris. "The Last Outlaw." *GQ*, November 2005. http://www.gq.com/.

Hemphill, Paul. *Lovesick Blues: The Life of Hank Williams.* New York: Penguin, 2005.

Hickey, Dave. "Notes on Kris Kristofferson 1968–1974." *Country Music*, September 1974, 30.

Hughes, Rob. "Kris Kristofferson: Troubadour Writing on into the Sunset." *Telegraph*, December 4, 2012. http://www.telegraph.co.uk/.

Hutchinson, Lydia. "Jimmy Webb's Story behind 'The Highwayman.'" *Performing Songwriter* 100, August 15, 2012. http://performingsongwriter.com/.

———. "Kristofferson's 'Me and Bobby McGee.'" *Performing Songwriter* 107, June 20, 2013. http://performingsongwriter.com/.

Jennings, Waylon, with Lenny Kaye. *An Autobiography.* New York: Warner, 1996.

Jordan, Rosa. "Kris Kristofferson: Interview." *Progressive*, September 1991. http://www. rosajordan.com/.

Kramer, Michael J. *The Republic of Rock: Music and Citizenship in the Sixties Counterculture.* New York: Oxford University Press, 2013.

Kris Kristofferson: His Life and Work. Directed by Paul Joyce. Forked River, NJ: Kultur International Films, 1993.

Kristofferson, Kris. Interviewed by Ken Paulson. *Speaking Freely*, First Amendment Center, November 14, 2003.

———. Interviewed by Miriam O'Callaghan. National Television and Radio Broadcasting (Ireland), July 8, 2010.

———. Interviewed by William Welfare. *Rolling Stone*, March 26, 2014. http://www.rollingstone.co.za/.

Lange, Jeffrey L. *Smile When You Call Me a Hillbilly: Country Music's Struggle for Respectability.* Athens: University of Georgia Press, 2004.

Langer, Andy. "Q&A with Kris Kristofferson." *Esquire*, February 27, 2006. http://www.esquire.com/.

Leigh, Spencer. "Kris Kristofferson Talks to Spencer Leigh." *Spencer Leigh*, June 28, 2004. http://www.spencerleigh.demon.co.uk/.

Lewis, Randy. "Kris Kristofferson Is 'Feeling Mortal.'" *Los Angeles Times*, January 23, 2013. http://articles.latimes.com/.

———. "Kris Kristofferson: Pop and Country's Semi-Tough Veteran." *Pop and Hiss: The L.A. Times Music Blog.* April 18, 2009. http://latimesblogs.latimes.com/.

Leydon, Joe. "Son of Nashville." *Cowboys and Indians Magazine*, September 2011. http://www.cowboysindians.com/.

Lornell, Kip. *Exploring American Folk Music: Ethnic, Grassroots, and Regional Traditions in the United States.* 3rd ed. Jackson: University Press of Mississippi, 2012.

Malone, Bill C., and Jocelyn R. Neal. *Country Music, USA.* 3rd rev. ed. Austin: University of Texas Press, 2010. (Malone is the preeminent country music historian.)

Margolis, Lynne. "Kris Kristofferson: On Record." *American Songwriter*, April 2, 2013. http://www.americansongwriter.com/.

McCall, Cheryl. "Can't Keep Kris Down." *People* 16, no. 10, September 7, 1981.

McClintock, Jack. "Just a Good Ole Rhodes Scholar: Making It through the Night with Kris Kristofferson." *Playboy* 18, no. 9, March 1975, 95, 122–70, 171–75.

Miller, Stephen. *Kristofferson: The Wild American.* London: Omnibus Press, 2010. (Miller's biography, though factually incomplete, is the only one written on Kristofferson, and he laments Kristofferson's lack of cooperation.)

Nelson, Paul. "Kris Kristofferson: *Easter Island*." *Rolling Stone*, April 20, 1978, 71.

Nelson, Steffie. "Dennis Hopper's *The Last Movie* Screens at Paris Photo." *T Magazine, New York Times*, April 28, 2014.

NPR staff. "Kris Kristofferson on Writing for—and Outliving—His Idols." NPR, February 3, 2013. http://www.npr.org/.

Oermann, Robert. *America's Music: The Roots of Country.* Atlanta: Turner Publications, 1996.

———. *Behind the Grand Ole Opry Curtain: Tales of Romance and Tragedy.* New York: Center Street, 2008.

Patterson, John. "I Was Killing Myself." *Guardian*, March 4, 2008. http://www.theguardian.com/.

Peterson, Richard. *Creating Country Music: Fabricating Authenticity.* Chicago: University of Chicago Press, 1997.

Pierson, Frank. "My Battles with Barbra and Jon." *New York*, November 15, 1976.

Pinkston, David. *Kris Kristofferson: Breakthrough.* DVD. Nashville: Oh Boy Records, 2004.

Pipkin, Turk. "Kris Kristofferson Is Still Living His Epic Life." *Culture Blog. Esquire*, May 12, 2014. http://www.esquire.com/.

Price, Deborah Evans. "Kris Kristofferson, Setting High Standards; and Continues to Learn About Himself and His Craft." *American Songwriter*, November 18, 2004. http://www.americansongwriter.com/.

Rabin, Nathan. "Week 27: Kris Kristofferson, Silver-Tongued Devil." *AV Club*, February 9, 2010. http://www.avclub.com/.

Reid, Graham. "Kris Kristofferson Interviewed (2005): Rebel with a Scholarship." *Wide Angle*, September 2, 2008. http://www.elsewhere.co.nz/. First published August 2005 in *New Zealand Herald*.

Rensin, David. "Kris Kristofferson." *Country Music*, September 1974, 25–32.

Rezos, Ray. "Kristofferson." *Rolling Stone*, November 1970, 38.

Rose, Charlie. "Interview with Kris Kristofferson." *Charlie Rose*. VHS. New York: CBS, 2009.

Ruhlmann, William. Review of *Easter Island* (1978). *Allmusic*. Accessed December 18, 2014. http://www.allmusic.com/.

———. Review of *Music from Songwriter* (1984). *Allmusic*. Accessed December 18, 2014. http://www.allmusic.com/.

———. Review of *Shake Hands with the Devil* (1979). *Allmusic*. Accessed December 18, 2014. http://www.allmusic.com/.

———. Review of sound track to *A Star Is Born* (1976). *Allmusic*. Accessed December 18, 2014. http://www.allmusic.com/.

Schneider, Jason. "Kris Kristofferson: The Pilgrim's Progress." *Timeline*, Exclaim.ca, September 26, 2009. http://exclaim.ca/.

Self, Philip. *Guitar Pull: Conversations with Country Music's Legendary Songwriters*. Nashville: Cypress Moon, 2002.

Silverman, Jonathan. *Nine Choices: Johnny Cash and American Culture*. Amherst: University of Massachusetts Press, 2010.

Streissguth, Michael. *Outlaw: Waylon, Willie, Kris, and the Renegades of Nashville*. New York: HarperCollins, 2013.

They Called Us Outlaws. Documentary. Kris Kristofferson interviewed by Sean Geadelmann. Austin: Country Music Hall of Fame and Museum, 2013.

Thibodeaux, Ron. "He Made It through the Night." *New Orleans Times-Picayune*, November 29, 2006.

Troubadours: Carole King/James Taylor and the Rise of the Singer-Songwriter. Documentary. *American Masters*, season 25, episode 2. Directed by Morgan Neville. PBS. Aired March 2, 2011. Cambridge, MA: Hear Music, 2011.

Williams, Paul. Interviewed by Carl Wiser. *Songwriter Interviews* (blog). Songfacts, June 1, 2007. http://www.songfacts.com/.

Willman, Chris. *Rednecks and Bluenecks: The Politics of Country Music*. New York: New Press, 2005.

Willson, Brian. *Blood on the Tracks: The Life and Times of S. Brian Willson*. Oakland, CA: PM Press, 2011.

Wordsworth, William. *Lyrical Ballads, 1800*. Edited by R. L. Brett and A. R. Jones. London: Methuen, 1963.

FURTHER LISTENING

KRISTOFFERSON

1970 (Monument)

Blame It on the Stones
To Beat the Devil
Me and Bobby McGee
The Best of All Possible Worlds
Help Me Make It through the Night
The Law Is for the Protection of the People
Casey's Last Ride
Just the Other Side of Nowhere
Darby's Castle
For the Good Times
Duvalier's Dream
Sunday Mornin' Comin' Down

These songs, previously recorded individually by A-1 artists, had popularized Kris Kristofferson's songs; however, when recorded in his voice, sales were minimal. When Janis Joplin's recording of "Me and Bobby McGee" skyrocketed after her death, Kristofferson's album was rereleased as *Me and Bobby McGee* and fared much better.

THE SILVER TONGUED DEVIL AND I

1971 (Monument)

The Silver Tongued Devil and I
Jody and the Kid
Billy Dee
Good Christian Soldier
Breakdown (A Long Way from Home)
Loving Her Was Easier (Than Anything I'll Ever Do Again)
The Taker
When I Loved Her
The Pilgrim, Chapter 33
Epitaph (Black and Blue)

"The Silver Tongued Devil and I," "The Taker," and "The Pilgrim" seemed to provide glimpses of Kristofferson's complexity and dark side that had not emerged in previous songs.

BORDER LORD

1972 (Monument)

Josie
Burden of Freedom
Stagger Mountain Tragedy
Border Lord
Somebody Nobody Knows
Little Girl Lost
Smokey Put the Sweat on Me
When She's Wrong
Getting By High and Strange
Kiss the World Goodbye

The most persistent belief in Kristofferson's songs is that freedom exacts a heavy burden. He had recently named his band the Borderlords.

JESUS WAS A CAPRICORN

1972 (Monument)

Jesus Was a Capricorn (Owed to John Prine)
Nobody Wins
It Sure Was (Love)
Enough for You
Help Me
Jesse Younger?
Give It Time to Be Tender
Out of Mind, Out of Sight
Sugar Man
Why Me

"Why Me" transformed this album into the highest grossing of all Kristofferson's albums; it reflects a religious experience prompted by grief and guilt about his family.

HIGHWAYMAN (WITH JOHNNY CASH, WAYLON JENNINGS, AND WILLIE NELSON)

1985 (Columbia)

Highwayman
The Last Cowboy Song
Jim, I Wore a Tie Today
Big River
Committed to Parkview
Desperados Waiting for a Train
Deportee (Plane Wreck at Los Gatos)
Welfare Line
Against the Wind
The Twentieth Century Is Almost Over

The first Highwayman album reached platinum designation with Jimmy Webb's title track that suggests reincarnation of past Americans.

THIRD WORLD WARRIOR

1990 (Mercury)

The Eagle and the Bear
Third World Warrior
Aguila del Norte
The Hero
Don't Let the Bastards Get You Down
Love of Money
Third World War
Jesse Jackson
Mal Sacate
Sandinista

This much-criticized album of protest against the U.S. government's encroachment in Central America effectively halted his recording career for six years.

THIS OLD ROAD

2006 (New West Records)

This Old Road
Pilgrim's Progress
The Last Thing to Go
Wild American
In the News
Burden of Freedom
Chase the Feeling
Holy Creation
The Show Goes On

Thank You for a Life
Final Attraction

This album marked Kristofferson's comeback in 2006. Many of the songs had been written and recorded years earlier but were now approached from a perspective that indicated his maturation.

FURTHER WATCHING

Cisco Pike (1972). Kristofferson's first real film part was one opposite Gene Hackman, a crooked cop. The sound track featured several of the tracks from Kristofferson's first album.

Pat Garrett and Billy the Kid (1973). With this film, Kristofferson, playing Billy the Kid, began his association with director Sam Peckinpah. Kristofferson persuaded Bob Dylan to join him in the film, and Dylan wrote the sound track that includes "Knocking at Heaven's Door."

Alice Doesn't Live Here Anymore (1974). In Martin Scorsese's acclaimed film about a woman who suddenly becomes a widow, Ellen Burstyn heads for California and goes bust in Phoenix, where she begins waitressing and meets sensitive rancher Kristofferson.

The Sailor Who Fell from Grace with the Sea (1976). In this film Kristofferson plays opposite Sarah Miles, a widowed mother, in a passionate love affair that troubles her young son. Based on a novel by Japanese author Yukio Mishima, the film includes Kristofferson's song "Sea Dream" on the sound track.

A Star Is Born (1976). Costarring opposite Barbra Streisand, Kristofferson plays a doomed self-destructive singer and sings none of his own songs but those by Streisand and Paul Williams. Critics hated it, but it went on to earn nearly $90 million.

Heaven's Gate (1980). The $42 million western based on the Johnson County Wars in nineteenth-century Wyoming crashed at the box office because of overruns and delays. Bad press afflicted Kristofferson's acting career for several years.

Songwriter (1984). A welcome opportunity during a low ebb in his life, Kristofferson was invited by his friend, Willie Nelson, to costar in his film about his experiences in the country music industry. Each wrote half the music in a film that was very well reviewed.

Trouble in Mind (1985). This stylized, somewhat futuristic film about an ex-con recently released from prison was helmed by Alan Rudolph, who also directed *Songwriter* and who thought Kristofferson was perfect for this film. Kristofferson wrote the title song.

Lone Star (1996). Kristofferson plays the part of a vicious Texas sheriff with consummate skill. Viewers and critics were surprised by his level of character interpretation.

Blade (1998). This is the first of three films in which Kristofferson plays the role of Abraham Whistler, vampire tracker. The films have developed a cult following.

INDEX

ABOUT THE AUTHOR

Mary G. Hurd is retired from East Tennessee State University, where she was director of film studies and a member of the English department faculty. She created the university's film studies minor, teaching classes on film and on American literature. She is the author of *Women Directors and Their Films* (2007) and many articles and reviews. She lives with her husband and daughter in northeast Tennessee.